50
HEIRLOOM
BUTTONS
to Make

—— NANCY NEHRING ——

photography by Marcus Tullis

50 HEIRLOOM BUTTONS to Make

NANCY NEHRING

photography by Marcus Tullis

The Taunton Press

Taunton
BOOKS & VIDEOS

for fellow enthusiasts

First printing: January 1996
Second printing: December 1996
Printed in the United States of America

A THREADS Book
THREADS® is a trademark of The Taunton Press, Inc.,
registered in the U.S. Patent and Trademark Office.

The Taunton Press, 63 South Main Street, Box 5506,
Newtown, CT 06470-5506

Library of Congress Cataloging-in-Publication Data

Nehring, Nancy.
    50 Heirloom buttons to make/Nancy Nehring.
        p.   cm.
    "A Threads book"—T.p. verso.
    ISBN 1-56158-146-1
    1. Buttons. 2. Button craft.
    I. Title.
TT57.N45   1996   95-51690
646'.19—dc20   CIP

Contents

Introduction

For most sewers, buttons come last. If they think about buttons at all, they're usually store-bought. But buttons can add a most distinctive touch to a garment. And whether you sew or not, there are a host of interesting button-making techniques that are fairly easy to learn and do.

Buttons should be a design element, not an afterthought in clothing design. Although buttons are used on garments for functional reasons, they usually command a central, eye-focusing location, so they should be chosen to complement a garment. I don't advocate that every garment be centered around its buttons, although this is possible—recall Elsa Schiaparelli's circus jacket featuring carousel horse buttons, or Christian Francis Roth's breakfast suit featuring sunny-side-up eggs with large yellow buttons as yolks. But neither should a garment be taken to a fabric store and buttons picked on the basis of which are the least distracting or offensive.

How do you find good buttons when the selection at most stores is limited to plain styles and basic colors? Often the answer lies in making buttons yourself, just as I do. Making my own buttons gives me complete control over style, shape, color, texture, and size.

Because button-making is an extension of my interests in clothing design and fabric embellishment, my buttons are fashioned from the same fabrics, threads, and trims that I am already familiar with. Techniques for making buttons are also familiar: sewing, embroidery, crochet, and braid work. I can create an infinite variety of buttons by changing threads and stitches. If you are a designer, a sewer, a costumer, or a needlecrafts person, you will appreciate not having to learn new skills or buy new materials to make these buttons. If you are not, the small scale of a button-making project makes it easy to approach.

My inspiration for the buttons featured here comes from my collection of original Victorian thread, braid, and fabric buttons made in cottage industries in the last half of the 19th century. These buttons were tiny works of art used to embellish dresses. A dress might use upwards of 30 of these buttons for trimming, even though the dress itself usually closed with hooks and eyes!

The buttons in this book make up quickly and easily, some in as few as 15 minutes each. I often wasted much more time just driving from store to store to look at uninspiring buttons I would never buy.

Don't expect to reproduce the buttons here exactly, of course. Threads, braids, and other materials used change from season to season. The examples and directions I've included should be used only as guides in selecting appropriate techniques and materials. You'll have the greatest fun selecting your own and in making buttons customized to match your own clothes. Enjoy!

Skill levels

Basic skills required. EASY

Intermediate skills required. MODERATE

Advanced skills required. CHALLENGING

Materials and Techniques

The key to making great-looking buttons is to think small: Choose fine threads and closely woven fabrics. A button worked in 4-ply yarn that ends up 2 in. wide will look sloppy, but the same button worked in a fine thread on a ½-in. mold will be quite elegant.

Buttons have two major components: a mold and a decorative cover. The mold must be firm so that the button will not slip back through the buttonhole after it is fastened. The decorative cover simply makes the mold a pleasure to use and to look at. Patterns for decorative covers in needle lace, crochet, braid work, fabric, and ribbon work are given here.

Buttons must be proportionate to the garment on which they are being used. Three variables can be adjusted to make an attractive button that looks good on your garment: thread, cord or braid thickness or fabric weave; mold size; and pattern. In general, it's best to pick a mold size and thread or fabric that are appropriate for the garment and then adjust the patterns given in this book so that the finished work fits the mold and looks good.

If possible, make a button before making the buttonholes on your garment. The materials used to create the button may add a substantial amount to the size of the button mold, even when the finest threads are used. Plan on making two or three test buttons to get the mold, the thread, and the pattern working together to your liking.

Adjusting patterns to fit different-size molds often involves a little experimentation, and each type of button requires a different method of attack. Fabric buttons, for example, usually require just a different-size circle of fabric to be cut. On many of the thread and braid patterns, the number of spokes or wraps can be increased or decreased to show off the pattern to full advantage. These patterns can also be adjusted by increasing or decreasing the number of rounds each pattern section makes over the spokes or by eliminating or creating new pattern sections. Crochet buttons can be changed in size by changing the hook and thread size, or by increasing or deleting rounds, especially outer rounds of single crochet.

Selecting Materials

Buttons may be made of fabric, thread, cord, or braid. If you use fabric, your choice of material will usually be dictated by the fabric used in the garment. Thin fabrics, where see-through might be a problem, can be underlined with a second layer of the same fabric or a lining fabric. Thin fabrics may also be fused to lightweight interfacing. Heavy fabrics are very difficult to manipulate into buttons and may require that you choose a coordinating fabric.

Thread and braid buttons are more durable than you might think. A set of buttons made out of cotton or linen thread can last as long as the garment it is on. The buttons can be washed and dried on the garment if the thread, mold, and other components are chosen accordingly. The buttons, even if buttoned and unbuttoned each time the garment is put on or taken off, will wear at about the same rate as the fabric of the garment. Remember, the thread in the buttons is much thicker than the thread in the garment fabric.

Threads of many types, even those designed for other purposes, often can be made into striking buttons. Try silk buttonhole twist: Even though expensive, it takes only a few yards for a button, and the luster is wonderful. Rayon machine embroidery thread (Sulky, Altazar) produces a button with a silklike luster, and the color selection is excellent. Linen threads for lace-making produce strong, durable buttons, although the color selection is limited. I have even unraveled thread from one end of yard goods to make matching buttons. Don't be afraid to try other threads. Even if you don't like the button, you won't be out much in terms of cost or time because a button requires so little of either!

Many different types of cord and braid can be used to make buttons. Generally, the smaller the button, the finer the material you will want to use. Cord or braid may be chosen to match other trim on a garment. For a finer button, you might pick apart a braid and use just one of its cords. Yarn can be substituted for cord or braid and used to make matching buttons for knitted garments. You can sometimes separate the plies of the yarn and use a single ply for a more delicate look and more durable button.

I generally stitch my buttons together. I resort to hot glue only when I am applying some braids and beads. Twisted braid, once cut to length, unravels instantly, and it is nearly impossible to stitch all the little threads down permanently. And beads sometimes just don't have enough holes in them, or the holes may not be in the right places, so glue is the only answer.

Types of Button Molds

Most buttons require some type of mold to support the handwork. The mold shape will affect the look of a finished button and how easily you can make it (especially with a button made directly on the mold). Most buttons are round, but even a round button has a variety of edge shapes that affect the look of the button. Round, half-round, knife, and flat edges are common (see the drawing below left).

Try to choose a mold material that can be cleaned in the same manner as your garment. If that's not possible, there are ways to make the button removable (see the sidebar below).

TRADITIONAL MOLD SHAPES

Side View

Round
Half-round
Knife
Square

The shape of the mold plays an important role in the finished look of a button.

Making Removable Buttons

If the buttons you make can't be cleaned, design them to be removable. Three methods work well. The simplest is to use a special button pin that looks like a safety pin with a bump on the outer side. A second method is to sew the handmade button to a small, flat, two-hole plastic button, adding a short shank to the handmade button if it doesn't have one. Then make two buttonholes: a small one on the button side to fit the plastic button, a larger one on the buttonhole side to fit the handmade button. Then just button the plastic button to the button side of the garment and the handmade button to the buttonhole side. A third method works well for a long row of buttons. Sew the buttons to a strip of flesh-colored cloth the length of the garment opening, spacing them as the pattern indicates. Make buttonholes to fit the handmade buttons on both sides of the garment. Position the strip under both layers of the garment, and button through the matching sets of buttonholes.

Commercial button molds

Commercial button molds—two-part metal or nylon—for self-covered buttons are readily available and come in various sizes and shapes. Half-round molds are slightly domed and are the most common shape. Flat molds, with a flat top surface and square edge, are also available. Sizes range from line 18 (7/16 in.) to line 100 (2½ in.). Metal molds are strong yet lightweight. Nylon molds are a little more flexible and will accommodate slightly heavier fabrics.

Disks

Some buttons require a hole in the center of the mold, but this type of mold is not readily available commercially. Instead, I use wood or bone disks. You may find wooden toy parts that can be adapted to this use (for sources of toy parts, see p. 108). Also, disk beads with a knife edge in either wood or bone can occasionally be found in bead shops.

Rings

Small metal or plastic rings can also be used as button molds. Some fabric stores and upholstery suppliers stock ½-in. or 9/16-in. brass rings for café curtains. Larger sizes are more difficult to locate, because you must use rolled or stamped brass rings. (Avoid the cast brass rings available in fabric and craft stores; they are too heavy and have a slit in them that the thread slips through.) For larger buttons, you can use plastic rings if you can't locate brass rings, but plastic rings are thicker and make a chunky button. For some buttons you may be able to make rings from sheet plastic or by soldering jump rings (used for making jewelry) closed.

Stuffed-ball molds

Some buttons call for a hard, dense center of fabric or stuffing as a mold. These types of molds—called stuffed-ball molds—are easy to make. First cut circles or squares of bonded or sheet stuffing all the same size to ensure that your buttons are all the same size. Then cut circles of fabric for the covering according to the directions with the button. With a double strand of quilting thread, work an in-and-out running stitch 1/8 in. from the edge of the fabric. Finger-press the 1/8-in. edge toward the center along the stitching line. Wad up the stuffing and pack it in the center of the fabric as you pull up on the running stitch.

Just before the running stitch closes, press on the ball to see if it has enough stuffing. The amount you need depends on the type of stuffing you use. Some stuffing materials pack down better than others. I like cotton quilt batting, which packs tighter than polyester. Pack the stuffing tightly to form a firm ball. The blunt tip of a crochet hook can be used to stuff a ball even more tightly. To finish, use the points of a sharp pair of embroidery scissors to tuck the 1/8-in. edge inside

Button molds. Clockwise from upper left: stuffed-ball molds, wood molds, brass and plastic rings, rim molds, plastic and metal molds for covered buttons, plastic rings for bullions (on crochet hook); other materials: mat board, cork, and old buttons. Center: bone and wood disk molds.

along the finger-pressed edge. Pull the thread tight to gather the fabric around and tie it off to form a ball. If the back needs a more secure closing, work a herringbone stitch over the opening, as shown in the drawing below.

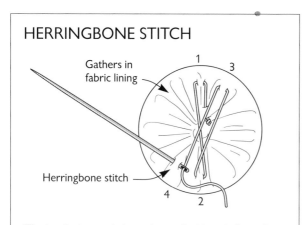

HERRINGBONE STITCH

Gathers in fabric lining

Herringbone stitch

1 3
4 2

The herringbone stitch can be worked in a circle to close the back of a stuffed ball or tighten a lining.

Other materials for molds

Beads, old buttons, bottle caps, champagne corks (which are easily sanded to any shape), or steel washers could all be used as molds to give a wide variety of shapes to your buttons. You can even create shapes from stacked mat board or other thin materials.

A few buttons discussed in this book require no mold at all. The form for this type of button is retained by a built-up, dense center of thread, braid, or cord, which becomes stiff enough to act as a mold.

Lining Options

You'll need to line a mold if your needlework does not fully cover the button, or if the top fabric is so thin that the mold shows through. Your best choices for this job are either lining fabric or Japanese flat embroidery silk (for sources of Japanese flat embroidery silk, see pp. 108-109).

Lining a mold with fabric

For commercial molds, cut the lining fabric according to the package directions. With a single strand of quilting thread and a needle, work a simple in-and-out running stitch ⅛ in. from the outer edge all around the fabric circle. Place the mold, front-side down, in the center of the fabric circle. Pull on the end of the thread to gather the outer edge of the fabric over the back of the mold. Tie off. Do not attach the back yet, except for crocheted buttons. After placing the final fabric or needlework on the button and attaching the back on your first sample button, pull hard on the shank to see if the back pops off. If it does, include another layer of fabric with the lining to tighten the back so that it won't pull off.

For other types of molds, begin by cutting a circle of lining fabric just over twice the diameter of the mold, plus its depth. With a single strand of quilting thread and a needle, work a simple in-and-out running stitch ⅛ in. from the outer edge all around the fabric circle. Place the mold, front-side down, in the center of the fabric circle. Pull on the end of the thread to gather the outer edge of the fabric over the mold and to the center back of the mold. Tie off the thread.

If the lining is not smooth and tight on the mold, work a herringbone stitch in a circle on the back until the lining fabric is smooth on the front of the mold. To do this with the same thread, take a stitch in a gather of the fabric about halfway between the center and the outer edge. Cross the center back to the opposite side of the button, take the next stitch in a gather of the fabric, and pull the thread snug. Again cross the center back of the mold, rotate the button slightly clockwise to the next gather, take a stitch, and pull up on the thread. Continue crossing the center back, rotating to the next gather, taking a stitch, and pulling up on the thread around the button until the lining fabric is smooth on the front of the button. Then tie off the thread.

Lining a mold with embroidery silk

A very elegant satinlike lining can be made by wrapping Japanese flat embroidery silk around a mold in a clockwise pattern, covering the mold completely. The mold for this lining must have a hole in the center. Hold the beginning tail at the center back and wrap the flat silk in a 12 o'clock to 6 o'clock, 1 o'clock to 7 o'clock pattern, with each wrap just touching the last one, until the mold is fully covered (see the drawing below). Cut the silk, leaving a 6-in. tail. Then thread the tail onto a tapestry needle. Go up through the center hole, over the area where the wraps cross at the front center and down through the hole. Tie off on the back and cut. With your fingernail, stroke the flat silk to straighten it, and cover any little gaps where the mold shows through.

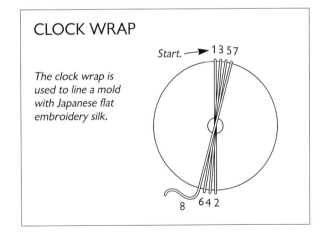

CLOCK WRAP

The clock wrap is used to line a mold with Japanese flat embroidery silk.

Start. → 1 3 5 7

8   6 4 2

Backing Your Button

Once you have finished the front of your button, you have to decide how to deal with the back. If you used a commercial mold, you may want to cover its shiny back. If you used something other than a commercial mold, chances are you have a button with an ugly back and no shank. Here are your finish options.

Covering a commercial back

Commercial button backs can be covered with lining fabric to give a finished look. Cut a circle of thin lining fabric a little less than twice the diameter of the back. Fold the fabric in quarters, and at the tip (the center of the circle when the fabric is unfolded), make a tiny snip. Unfold the fabric and put a drop of fabric sealer on the cut. With a single strand of quilting thread and a needle, work a simple in-and-out running stitch ⅛ in. from the outer edge all around the fabric circle. Place the back, shank-side down, in the center of the fabric circle and push the shank through the cut. Pull on the end of the thread to gather the outer edge of the fabric over the inside back. Tie off. Check the front of the button and decide which direction you want the shank to line up. Attach the back according to package directions.

A covered commercial back can be used with other molds also. Instead of attaching it to the front that the mold comes with, blind-stitch the outer edge to other buttons to make a back that conceals everything.

Making a solid back

If a commercial back won't work for your button, you can make your own from a solid disk of plastic or cardboard and add a woven shank. Cut a circle of plastic or lightweight cardboard a little smaller than the diameter of your button. Cover the circle with fabric, using the same technique as for the commercial back, but without snipping a hole for the shank. Then apply a woven shank (see "Adding a woven shank" on the facing page), sewing the short ends of the rectangle through the lining and the plastic or cardboard. Check the front of the button and decide which direction you want the shank to line up. To attach the back to the button, stitch around the outer edge of the covered circle.

Making a thread back

Some buttons have a hollow center in the back and require a special treatment. Make a back for these buttons by stitching in a clock pattern across the hollow back into the braid or fabric around the back edge of the

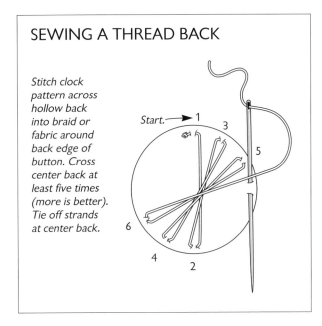
Adding a woven shank

If you have a fabric or lined button, you can add a woven shank made from thread. A shank is especially nice when the button is going on thick fabric. The extra height of the shank keeps the button from puckering the outer fabric. Centered on the back of the button, stitch two rounds of a rectangle using heavy thread, with the short sides under the lining and the long sides on top (see the drawing below). Weave back and forth in a figure-eight pattern over the long sides of the rectangle, passing the thread down at the center between the two sides of the rectangle, up over the outer edge, and back down at the center. Tie off.

button; stitch from 12 o'clock to 6 o'clock, 1 o'clock to 7 o'clock, and so on, as shown above. You'll want to cross the center back at least five times for strength; more is better. Secure the thread by knotting over the strands at the center back. Use the center back as an anchor to sew the button to your garment.

WEAVING A SHANK

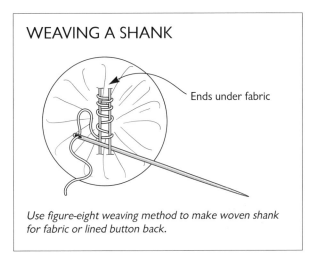

Ends under fabric

Use figure-eight weaving method to make woven shank for fabric or lined button back.

Needle-Lace Buttons

Needle lace, fashioned with a fine thread and needle, is worked or mounted on a mold to create needle-lace buttons. The mold for a needle-lace button can be either a ring or a disk. The ring buttons have a light, airy look, while the disk buttons have a heavy, tailored look.

Although virtually unseen on modern garments, needle-lace buttons have a long history. During the Middle Ages, after the establishment of artisan guilds—associations of merchants or craftsmen with similar skills or trades—button makers belonged to the same guild as lace makers, and naturally, lace-making techniques were incorporated into buttons. In France, buttons commissioned by the nobility were created using silk and gold threads and were encrusted with metal spangles and precious stones. In 1642 one of the masterpieces required for guild membership in Hungary was a set of buttons made of silk fabric and gold thread in a double heart shape.

In England and Germany from about 1650 to 1900, needle-lace buttons took another form. Cottage industries produced tens of thousands of buttons annually, using local resources such as linen from flax, horn molds from sheep, and silk from local growers. Such buttons were the cheapest to produce and were widely used on children's wear, women's blouses, and underwear. The buttons were exported or used by clothing manufacturers.

At the Great Exposition of 1851 in London, the Ashton button machine was introduced, which could mass-produce linen fabric-covered buttons. Within 10 years, makers of the cheap needle-lace buttons (such as Dorset buttons) were out of work. Production of more elaborate hand-wrought buttons began to wane also. By the end of World War I, mass production of cheap plastic buttons ended the handmade button industry, and improvements in production and the widespread use of plastics inverted the pricing structure for buttons. Plastic buttons became cheaper, and handmade buttons more expensive. Handmade buttons were so expensive, in fact, that the only ones used were those commissioned by Paris designers for their most expensive creations.

Needle lace can be made either on or off the mold. Because buttons usually are round, spokes radiating from the center of the button are used as the warp. The spokes may be used as a base for weaving, as in the Victorian woven buttons, or as corner anchors where the weft is woven through itself, as in Leek buttons. The number of spokes can vary greatly. If only a few spokes (say up to 20) are desired, the lace can be made directly on the mold. If many spokes (say over 20) are desired, the lace pattern can be better controlled off the mold, as in Teneriffe lace.

Needle-lace buttons require a rigid mold that won't deform during weaving. A mold is generally a ring or a solid disk with a small hole in the center. Some buttons require an opening in the center to pass threads from back to front. Historically, rings were of bone or wire, and disks were of bone or wood. Similar mold materials are available today with a little searching, but other less conventional molds can be used, such as old plastic buttons.

To make the spokes for any type of needle-lace button, one of two wrapping methods is used: the clock wrap or the X-wrap.

The Clock Wrap

The clock wrap produces radiating spokes to prepare for a woven decorative pattern. It is the most common spoke pattern used for buttons with lacy openings in the pattern. To execute a clock wrap, pull thread from the center back of the mold, across the edge, over the center front, across the opposite edge, and return to the center back. Rotate the mold slightly and repeat the procedure until you reach the desired number of spokes. Each wrap of thread across the face of the mold creates two spokes that extend from the center of the mold to an outside edge (see the drawing on the facing page).

When wrapping spokes on a disk mold, you may find that rotating the mold to position a new spoke will cause the thread to slip to one side of the back of the mold instead of across the center back. You can prevent slippage by wrapping the thread to the center back and then holding it there with your fingertip before rotating the mold to position the next spoke. After you have wrapped all of the spokes, hold them in place at the center back by working a cross-stitch over them where they intersect. Then anchor the spokes by passing the needle and thread to the front of the mold through the center hole. Come out in the V between two spokes. Count around one half of the spokes. Cross over the center to this V and pass the needle and thread through the center hole to the back. If the decorative weaving pattern starts at the front center, pass the needle and thread up to the top again, coming out in any V. You are now ready to start weaving the final pattern.

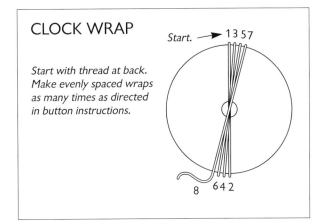

CLOCK WRAP

Start with thread at back. Make evenly spaced wraps as many times as directed in button instructions.

Start. → 1 3 5 7

8 6 4 2

The X-Wrap

The X-wrap is used on buttons where the entire surface of the mold will be covered with thread. Begin with the thread tail at center back. Wrap the thread over the edge, across the center front, over the opposite edge, returning to the center back. Repeat one, two or three more times as indicated in the instructions for the button you are working (see the drawing below). You can secure the first side of the X while wrapping the second side. Bring the thread just past the center back and hold it there with your fingertip. Rotate the mold 90°. As you wrap the thread around the mold one to four times again, wrap back toward the center of the mold. Wrap over the last half wrap of the first side, securing the first wraps and the turn. Work a cross-stitch over the threads at the center back and tie off. Make sure you tie the beginning tail in securely. The arms of the X will anchor the thread that covers the mold.

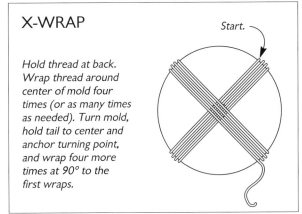

X-WRAP

Start.

Hold thread at back. Wrap thread around center of mold four times (or as many times as needed). Turn mold, hold tail to center and anchor turning point, and wrap four more times at 90° to the first wraps.

Dorset Buttons

Dorset buttons are probably the most widely known needle-lace buttons. They were made in a cottage industry in southern England from the early 1700s until about 1860. During the height of production, hundreds of thousands were made annually and shipped around the world. Women, men, and children were all employed in the industry. Employees were in such short supply that prisons and orphanages were contracted to make buttons. (The social justification was to teach these people a marketable skill.) For more information about the history of Dorset buttons, read *Dorset Buttons–Fact File* in the Helpful Books section on p. 109.

Many styles of Dorset buttons were produced using different mold materials and coverings. Both bone disks and wire rings were used for molds, and both fabric and thread were used for coverings. Four button styles using thread are described in this section. (One fabric style, called the Singleton, is described in detail on p. 100.) The buttons' names describe their patterns: crosswheel, bird's eye, basket, mite, knob. Similar patterns were sometimes developed in different communities in England but would be given different names. Sometimes a family would make an exclusive Dorset pattern, such as the Singleton.

Dorset ring buttons

Dorset ring buttons are among the most versatile of buttons. They can be made in any size, from ½ in. or less to 1¼ in. or more, and any thread or fine cord will work: crochet, lace-weight linen, fine tapestry wool, pearl cotton, buttonhole twist, and metallic braid. If you want to match a garment, you can unravel the end of yard goods or split yarn down to 1 ply.

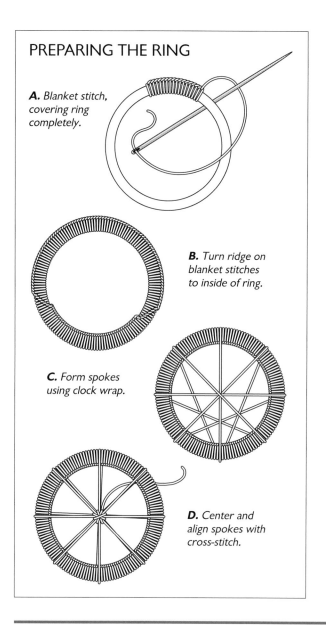

PREPARING THE RING

A. Blanket stitch, covering ring completely.

B. Turn ridge on blanket stitches to inside of ring.

C. Form spokes using clock wrap.

D. Center and align spokes with cross-stitch.

Dorset buttons: clockwise from upper left, Dorset knob, Dorset crosswheel, grindle, Dorset basket.

The most critical step in making a Dorset ring button is to center the spot where the spokes cross. If the crossing point is off center by even a little, the button will look crooked, and once you start weaving the pattern, you can't move the center.

Covering the rings All Dorset ring buttons begin by working a blanket stitch over the ring. Just the weaving patterns vary.

To cover a ring to make a Dorset button, you'll need:
- 9/16-in. brass ring
- 30/3 topstitching thread
- #24 tapestry needle.

Cut 2½ yd. of thread. Make sure you start with a long enough piece so that you don't have to add thread because it's difficult to make a join look neat. Tie thread onto ring with an overhand knot. Work blanket stitches, as shown in the drawing on p. 18.

Have the first few stitches cover the thread tail and then trim the tail. Pack the stitches closely so that the ring doesn't show. When you have covered the ring, slip the needle through the first stitch to hold first and last blanket stitches together. Turn the ridge of blanket stitches to the inside of the ring.

Next, make spokes across the center of the ring, using the clock wrap, as shown in the drawing on p. 18. Make as many spokes as you like, but six wraps for 12 spokes is a good number to start with. After making the last spoke, move to the center back of the button and work a cross-stitch over all of the spokes (both front and back) where they intersect at the center to align the front and back spokes. Tie thread but do not cut.

The front and back spokes should now line up and are treated as one for weaving. Weave over the front and back spokes using one of the following patterns. Then move the thread to center back and tie off. Sew the button onto the garment by passing the needle up through the button near the center, cross the center over the cross-stitch, and go back down through the button. If you prefer a shank, you can work a woven shank (see p. 13) using two spokes on each side of the button for anchors.

Dorset crosswheel

EASY

To make the sample in ecru on p. 19 (upper right), start at center front of the button and work one backstitch over each spoke all the way around. Fill the spokes out to the ring (drawing below). Lay thread back to the center of the button, catch a few threads, and tie off.

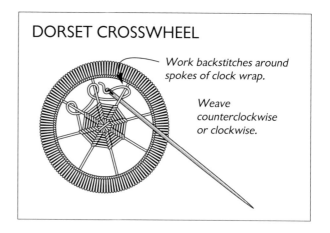

DORSET CROSSWHEEL

Work backstitches around spokes of clock wrap.

Weave counterclockwise or clockwise.

Dorset basket

EASY

To make one of the samples in the lower left corner on p. 19, begin at the center of the button. Backstitch over two spokes. Move forward four spokes. Backstitch over the two unused spokes. Continue completing the first round. On the second round, backstitch over the same pairs of spokes used in the first round. On the third round, move over one spoke. Backstitch over two spokes until all of the spokes are used. This will offset the backstitches between the second and third rounds by one spoke. The fourth round uses the same spokes as the third round. The fifth round is offset by one spoke again, and the pattern is repeated to fill the spokes (drawing below).

Variations of Dorset ring buttons

The basket and the crosswheel are just two variations of the Dorset ring button. But don't feel limited by these two choices. Variations are fairly simple to achieve. The drawing at right shows three different ring buttons, but you may also want to try the following:

- Combine other embroidery stitches for the central weaving pattern.
- Combine weaving stitches.
- Change thread color while weaving.
- Include beads on the spokes.
- Vary the number of spokes or lay down spokes asymmetrically.
- Vary the stitches over the spokes to create a pattern to coordinate with your garment.

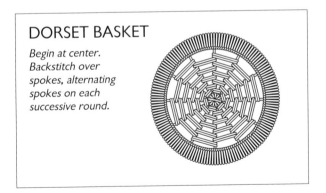

DORSET BASKET

Begin at center. Backstitch over spokes, alternating spokes on each successive round.

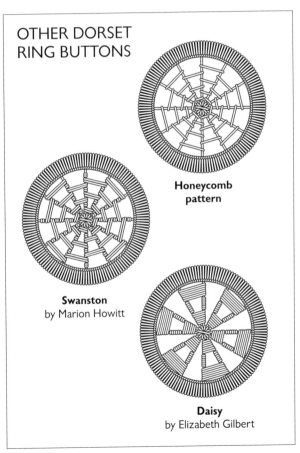

OTHER DORSET RING BUTTONS

Honeycomb pattern

Swanston
by Marion Howitt

Daisy
by Elizabeth Gilbert

Dorset knob MODERATE

The Dorset high top, a tall, conical version of the Dorset knob, was the first needle-lace button to be produced in southern England. The buttons were tiny, about 9mm in diameter at the base. High tops were used on men's waistcoats, including the one that King Charles I wore to his execution. Queen Victoria owned a gown lavishly trimmed with Dorset knobs.

When the Dorset button industry collapsed around 1860, the construction method for the Dorset knob was lost. In the 1970s, Elizabeth Gilbert of Wincanton, England, experimented with reproducing the knob. She finally resorted to picking apart a valuable antique to unravel its secrets. Originally, the mold was made of a wad of cloth held in a ball shape with glue. A small disk of horn resembling a modern-day sequin served as a base for the button.

The charm of the Dorset knob is in the ridges formed by the stitching. Use a relatively small thread for the size of the mold to achieve intricately plaited ridges. You can vary the number of ridges, but use enough so that the thread never travels more than ⅜ in. between ridges. The version described below uses a stuffed mold. Because it is difficult to stuff a large mold firmly, try to keep this button small. If you need a large knob, substitute a fabric-covered, high-domed wood mold.

For sample in tan on p. 19, you'll need:
- 1¾-in. circle of fabric to make a ⅝-in. stuffed mold
- 4 ft. 30/3 topstitching thread
- #7 embroidery needle.

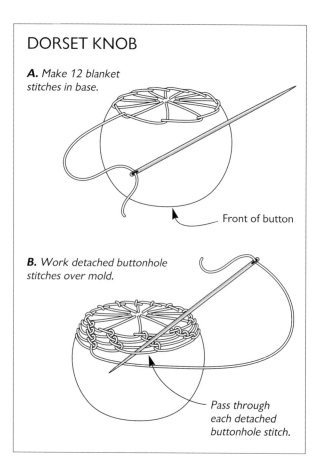

DORSET KNOB

A. *Make 12 blanket stitches in base.*

Front of button

B. *Work detached buttonhole stitches over mold.*

Pass through each detached buttonhole stitch.

Use the 1¾-in. circle of fabric to make a stuffed mold (see pp. 9-10). Thread the needle and knot the end of the thread. Make 12 blanket stitches around the closing of the stuffed mold, as shown in the drawing above. This will be the base, or back, of the button. Work one detached buttonhole stitch in each blanket stitch. Pull back on each detached buttonhole stitch so that the loop is aligned over the corner where two adjacent blanket stitches meet. Continue working detached buttonhole stitches around the mold, placing one in each stitch of the previous round. Again, pull back on the stitches so that the loops line up on top of each other. The stitches will form a ridge that spirals toward the center front. Near the center front you will run out of room to work more stitches. So pass the needle through each detached buttonhole stitch, then from the front center through the mold to the center back, and tie off. If you would like a shank, make a woven shank (see how on p. 13) across the back.

Grindle

MODERATE

Grindle is an old name for a stone. Although in terms of technique this button is in the same family as the Dorset buttons, there is no evidence that this particular style was made by the Dorset-button cottage industry. The original that I have is from early this century and has a paper mold (remember, paper was made from 100% cotton then). I have included it here because of the similarity of technique.

The surface of the grindle is worked the same as the center for a Dorset crosswheel: spokes covered with backstitches. As with the Dorset ring buttons, you can change the mold size, the number of spokes, and the weight, fiber content, and color of the thread to create a variety of buttons. You might also weave or embroider other threads over the backstitches. If you change mold or thread, begin with enough thread so that you don't have to add more. It's impossible to get a neat, clean join. For the mold, I use a ¾-in. axle cap made for toy wooden vehicles (cap sizes range from ¼ in. to ¾ in. in diameter—the cap sizes also are available in different heights). I drill a hole in the top of the cap so that I can pass the needle and thread through.

For sample in white on p. 19, you'll need:
- ¾-in.-diameter, ¾-in.-high domed wood mold
- 3 yd. #30 crochet cotton
- 2-in. circle of lining fabric to cover mold
- #24 tapestry needle.

Cut a 2-in. circle of lining fabric. Line the mold according to instructions on pp. 10-11. Tie off thread.

Thread #30 crochet cotton onto the tapestry needle. Knot thread and take two or three stitches through the lining near the center back to anchor the thread. Use the clock wrap (see drawing on p. 17) to make 12 spokes for weaving. With thread, cross-stitch over the spokes where they meet at the center back. Center the cross-stitch and knot, but don't cut the thread. To anchor spokes on the front, go from the back through the center hole and cross-stitch over the spokes where they meet in the front center. Pull tight but do not cut. If the spokes are not evenly spaced, the button will look lopsided, so pick up the spokes on front with the tip of your needle and align them.

To weave the pattern, backstitch around all 12 spokes until the mold is fully covered, as shown in the drawing on p. 20. Check spoke spacing each round, and adjust if necessary. Push the backstitches along the spokes toward the center if the lining shows between rounds. Knot the thread on back and cut. Sew through the center back of the button and through the garment fabric to attach the button to clothing, or add a woven shank (see p. 13).

Victorian Woven Buttons

Victorian woven buttons were used from about 1850 until 1920 on commercial and home-sewn garments. Home sewers could buy finished buttons on cards (as we buy buttons today) or in pieces that they could make up themselves. Several weaving stitches were used and combined in multiple ways to produce many different designs. The Victorian flag, flower, and star represent three of the most popular designs.

Like a Victorian needleworker, you can easily adapt these buttons to suit your garment. First choose an appropriate mold size. Next choose your cord. A very tight twist to the cord is essential to prevent the cord (and, therefore, the design) from being flattened as the weaving pulls the spokes tighter and tighter. I recommend Griffin silk bead cord because it produces the most historically accurate button. Choose a mold lining that either matches or coordinates with the garment fabric or silk cord. Then you can mix and match weaving patterns. For instance, if a pattern suggests backstitching for five rounds, and you are using the suggested cord but a larger mold, you might backstitch for seven rounds. Or you may prefer the blanket stitch instead of the loop stitch to finish your button.

Making a Victorian woven button

The general instructions for making the Victorian woven buttons featured here consist of weaving a decorative pattern on top of a lined mold. The mold must have a hole in the center through which to pass the needle and cord back and forth. Victorian woven buttons are all lined, and spokes are formed for weaving in a similar fashion. The main differences are in the weaving patterns. To make a sample button of a particular size, first use the chart below to determine the materials you'll need. Note that the design for some buttons requires a finer cord than others.

Materials List for Victorian Woven Buttons					
Finished button size	Wood mold size	Griffin silk bead cord size			Lining fabric diameter*
		Flag	Star	Flower	
1 in.	7/8 in.	4	4	6	2 in.
7/8 in.	3/4 in.	2	2	4	1 3/4 in.
3/4 in.	5/8 in.	1	1	2	1 1/2 in.

If you prefer, you can line the mold with Japanese flat embroidery silk (15 yd.) instead of lining fabric (see p. 11).

In addition, you'll need:
- 1 yd. quilting thread to match lining fabric
- #24 tapestry needle
- #7 embroidery or crewel needle
- needle grabber or small pliers

The first step for any Victorian woven button is lining the mold with fabric or flat silk (see pp. 10-11). Next, form the spokes that will be used as warp for the weaving. Unwind the silk cord and cut off the wire needle. Thread about 3 in. onto the embroidery needle. You will have to flatten the end of the cord to get it through the eye of the needle. Take two small stitches

Victorian woven buttons: clockwise from upper left, Victorian flower, Victorian star, Victorian flag.

through the lining near the center back, leaving a 1-in. tail to anchor the cord. Use the clock wrap (see the drawing on p. 17) to form spokes for the buttons, according to the directions for each button. Pass the cord back up through the center hole to the front. You are now ready to weave the desired patterns onto the front of the button. You may change to a tapestry needle now to make weaving easier.

Victorian flag

MODERATE

To make the sample in red on p. 24, form 12 spokes using the clock wrap. With needle and cord on the front of the button, begin weaving the pattern. Backstitch around all 12 spokes for five rounds to form the center pattern, as shown in drawing A (facing page). You may work either clockwise or counterclockwise.

Use an overcast stitch to form the flags. Begin the first flag using the last two spokes that you worked backstitches over (drawing B). Pass the cord over then under the two spokes four times. On these first two spokes, leave the overcast stitches loose. Then take one backstitch around the last spoke. Pass the cord under the next spoke right up next to the backstitches. Repeat the four overcast stitches using the spoke you just passed the cord under and the one from the last set of overcast stitches that you worked the backstitch around. The flag will form at an angle with one side up against the backstitches, and one side below the previously made flag. Continue around the button. When making the last flag, work the overcast stitches on the last spoke between the backstitches and the four overcast stitches of the first flag. Pass the cord along the spoke through the center of the first four overcast stitches to be in position to begin working the next pattern section.

The outer pattern consists of three rounds of reverse backstitches (drawing C). Work backstitches as in the first pattern section, but reverse the direction that you turn the mold. The cord between spokes will fall on top of the spokes instead of under them. When completed, pass the cord to the back of the button along a spoke.

The reverse backstitches are held in place with a blanket stitch. (If you've been using a tapestry needle, switch back to an embroidery needle.) Begin the blanket stitch by running the needle through the lining (fabric or flat silk) about a third of the way between the outer edge and center on the back of the button and positioned between two spokes. Move back to the front of the button and, with the needle pointed from the center to the outside edge of the button, make a blanket stitch over the three reverse backstitches. Pull snug to form a V in the reverse backstitches. How much you pull depends on how tightly you worked the reverse backstitches and on the look you want. Move to the back of the button again. Take a stitch under the lining in the same place as the first stitch to hold the blanket stitch in place (drawing D). Move to a position between the next two spokes and repeat. Continue working blanket stitches around the button. On the back, tie off, work a woven shank, if desired, and cut the cord.

VICTORIAN FLAG

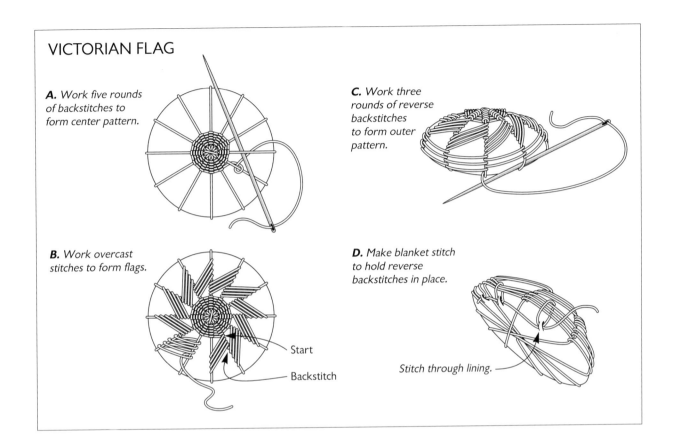

A. Work five rounds of backstitches to form center pattern.

C. Work three rounds of reverse backstitches to form outer pattern.

B. Work overcast stitches to form flags.

Start

Backstitch

D. Make blanket stitch to hold reverse backstitches in place.

Stitch through lining.

Tip: If you run out of silk cord, place the short cord along a spoke to the back of the button. Tie off. Attach a second cord to the back, place it along the same spoke back to the spot where you ran out of cord. On successive rounds, treat the spoke and the two cords that went to the back as one.

VICTORIAN FLOWER

A. Work overcast stitches to weave center pattern.

Move back to center.

Start.

B. Work reverse backstitches to create middle pattern.

C. Work blanket stitches.

D. Work loop stitch to hold reverse backstitches in place.

Stitch through lining.

Victorian flower   MODERATE

To make the sample in gray on p. 24, wrap 10 spokes using the clock wrap, then bring the needle and cord up through the center hole. To weave the center pattern, overcast two adjacent spokes six times each from the center out (drawing A, left). Don't pull the overcast stitches tight; allow the spokes to spread naturally. Move the cord back to the center of the button by placing it along one side of the overcast stitches, and overcast the next pair in the same manner. Repeat around the button. You will have five pairs of overcast spokes.

The middle pattern begins with three rounds of reverse backstitches (drawing B). On the fourth round, reverse backstitch over a spoke, work a blanket stitch over the three backstitches already in place (drawing C), then reverse backstitch over the next spoke, and continue around the button.

For the outside pattern, work three more rounds of reverse backstitches. The last three rounds are held in place by a loop stitch. (If you've been using a tapestry needle, switch to an embroidery needle.) On the back of the button, run the needle under the lining, coming up next to a spoke. Turn to the front of the button, pass the needle under the spoke above the last three rounds, move to the back again, and insert the needle under the lining on the other side of the spoke. Move to the next spoke, as shown in drawing D. Repeat around. On the back, tie off, work a woven shank, if desired, and cut the cord.

Victorian star   MODERATE

To make the sample in tan on p. 24, begin by wrapping 16 spokes, spacing them so that there are two spokes in each of eight positions, as shown in drawing A (facing page). Work a cross-stitch over the cords where they

VICTORIAN STAR

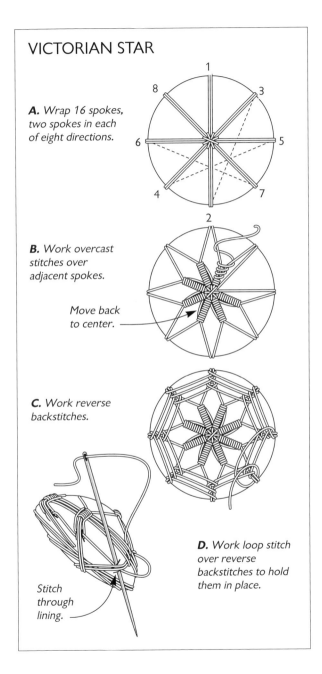

A. Wrap 16 spokes, two spokes in each of eight directions.

B. Work overcast stitches over adjacent spokes.

Move back to center.

C. Work reverse backstitches.

D. Work loop stitch over reverse backstitches to hold them in place.

Stitch through lining.

cross at the center back. To anchor the spokes on the front, bring the needle and cord to the front of the button through the center hole. Come out in the V between two pairs of spokes. Count around four pairs of spokes. Cross over the center to this V and pass the needle and cord through the center hole to the back. Pass the needle and cord up to the front again, coming out in any V. Pass the needle under one of a pair of spokes.

To weave the pattern, work overcast stitches around one spoke from each of two adjacent pairs 10 times from the center out (drawing B). Pull the overcast stitches tight so that the two spokes look like one. Move back to the center. The cord will lie to one side of the 10 overcast stitches you just made. Use the lone spoke and one spoke from the next pair and overcast these two spokes 10 times. Continue around the button until all eight pairs of spokes have been overcast.

To make the outer pattern, move to the edge by placing the silk cord along one spoke of the last pair overcast. Work a reverse backstitch over a pair of the original spokes—one spoke from each of two adjacent overcast pairs (drawing C). Continue around the button three times. Then work loop stitches to hold the reverse backstitches in place (drawing D). The loop stitch starts by taking a small stitch on the back of the button through the lining directly under a spoke. Loop the cord to the front of the button over the three reverse backstitches, under the spoke, and over the three reverse backstitches on the other side of the spoke. Complete the loop stitch by taking another stitch through the lining in the same place as the first stitch. Move to the next spoke on the back of the button and repeat. When the loop stitches are completed, tie off the cord. Work a woven shank, if desired, and cut the cord.

Shirtwaist Buttons

Shirtwaist buttons are often confused with Dorset buttons, although they originated in a different place and time. The buttons were used on Edwardian shirtwaists, coordinating well with the lightweight fabrics and lace trims popular between 1901 and 1910. As cleanliness began to assume more importance in people's lives, buttons had to stand up to "modern" cleaning methods of boiling and bleaching, and to new equipment such as wringers. Because they were made on heavy, flat metal rings, shirtwaist buttons could withstand the rigors of modern cleaning.

The wrapping method for shirtwaist buttons differs significantly from the wrapping method of Dorset buttons. On shirtwaist buttons the spokes are formed first, and the ring is covered last. These buttons used several variations on the theme to create different window and star patterns. The patterns require differing tensions on the thread as different parts of the pattern are wrapped, so shirtwaist buttons are more difficult to master.

These buttons attach to a garment by sewing up through the spokes, across the center cross-stitch, and back down through the spokes on the other side.

Lace shirtwaist

The most popular pattern for shirtwaist buttons, lace shirtwaist buttons were made in a variety of colors using the new colorfast aniline dyes, and in two-tone thread. The two-tone buttons had the inner spokes worked in white, and the outer blanket stitches in color. Cotton, silk, and linen threads were all used for this button style.

For the sample in champagne at right, you'll need:
- %16-in. brass ring
- 30/3 topstitching thread
- #24 tapestry needle.

First, cut 3½ yd. of thread. Tie the thread on the ring. Wrap the thread around the ring *tightly*, crossing center 10 times, and space the spokes evenly around the ring. End at center back (see drawing A on p. 32). This creates 20 spokes.

Next, form the circular window in the center using the spokes to anchor the wraps in this round. Counting the last spoke formed as spoke 1, count clockwise seven spokes (one-third the number of spokes, more or less) and wrap thread *loosely* from back to front, anchoring it on the far side of this spoke (see drawing B). Now go back (counterclockwise) one spoke past spoke 1. On the front of the button, wrap *loosely* on the far side of this spoke (see drawing C).

Tip: If you can't get the thread to anchor on the spokes, move down one or two more spokes (one-third the number of spokes plus one, or one-third

Shirtwaist buttons: star shirtwaist (in gold) and lace shirtwaist (in champagne).

LACE SHIRTWAIST

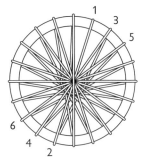

A. *Wrap across ring 10 times to form 20 spokes.*

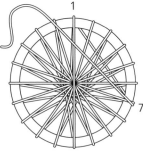

B. *From 1, wrap loosely around 7, from back to front, forming first angle wrap.*

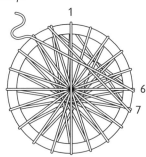

C. *Move back one spoke from 1 and wrap from back to front around 6 to form second angle wrap.*

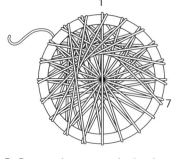

D. *Form angle wraps on both sides of spokes and make circular window in center.*

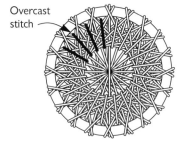

Overcast stitch

E. *Work overcast stitches over angle wraps to hold them in place.*

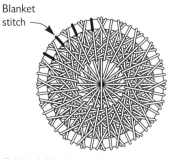

Blanket stitch

F. *Work blanket stitches over ring between wraps to fill ring.*

plus two). Continue moving over one spoke counterclockwise on each end of the wrap and wrap all the way around the ring. When you have made half of the angle wraps, the spoke that you want to use will already have one angle wrap anchored on it. Continue wrapping, anchoring the new wrap on the opposite side of the spoke from the existing wrap, as in drawing D. When you finish the angle wraps, there will be one wrap on each side of each spoke, making 20 sets of three threads.

Break off about 3 ft. of thread, and thread the needle. From the back, come up to the front near the center. Work an overcast stitch between each set of three threads catching only the angle wraps above the spokes, as shown in drawing E. Make the overcast stitch by pointing the needle from the outside toward the center under three angle wraps and then back over the top of the angle wraps to the next position.

Finally, add blanket stitches over the ring between the sets of three threads (see drawing F). Use as many stitches as you need to cover the ring (the sample here uses three). Keep the bar of the blanket stitch to the back of the button. Tie off thread at center.

Star shirtwaist

These instructions are for a six-point star, but you can use this method to work an eight-point star, too.

For the sample in gold on p. 31, you'll need:
- ½-in. brass ring
- 30/3 topstitching thread
- #24 tapestry needle.

Cut 1 yd. of thread and tie the thread onto the ring. Thread the needle onto the long end of the thread about 1 ft. Use the clock wrap to wrap three spokes tightly in each of three positions: 12 to 6, 8 to 2, and 10 to 4 o'clock, as shown in drawing A (right).

Form the sides of the star next. Using the spokes as anchors, loosely wrap three times from 8 to 4 o'clock, then three times from 10 to 6 o'clock, and continue around, making three wraps from 12 to 8, 2 to 10, 4 to 12 and 6 to 2 o'clock (see drawings B and C). Complete the pattern by passing the thread under the spoke and side at 6 o'clock when wrapping the last side. To finish the button, work five blanket stitches over the ring between two star points, and secure the angle wraps by working one blanket stitch over the intersection of the spoke and star sides, as in drawing D. Continue working blanket stitches around the button until completed. Tie thread off at center back.

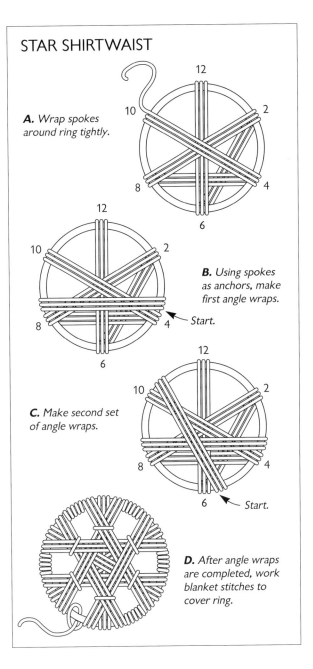

STAR SHIRTWAIST

A. Wrap spokes around ring tightly.

B. Using spokes as anchors, make first angle wraps.

Start.

C. Make second set of angle wraps.

Start.

D. After angle wraps are completed, work blanket stitches to cover ring.

Leek Buttons

Leek, England, was the center of another cottage button-making industry as early as 1645. Silk from Macclesfield and mohair from local goats were the main fibers used in the early leek buttons. But later versions of the buttons were made with just silk. Leek buttons remained popular into this century and had a commercial market until the 1920s. A few buttons were produced as late as 1950 to adorn robes of cardinals. Most of the buttons were dark and were used on men's vests and top coats.

The leek buttons described here are always wrapped from the corner anchors toward the center. Each round of thread is anchored by the previous round. Although these buttons carry the leek name, the drawing for the death's head appeared in *Denis Diderot's Encyclopédie* (ca. 1750), indicating that this type of button was also made in France (and probably elsewhere).

Death's head   CHALLENGING

This beautiful button has a somber name whose origin is unknown. For the death's head, use a mold with a knife edge and a hole in the center. I look for knife-edged wood or bone disk beads in bead stores, and pick them up whenever I find them. A thin mat board or plastic circle is a good alternative.

Because this button is made using a simple wrapping technique and no weaving, a variety of threads can be used. Thick or thin, soft or stiff all work well. Using this same technique, buttons can also be made with six or eight anchor points.

For sample in tan at left, you'll need:
- 1-in. knife edge wood disk mold
- 40/2 linen thread
- #24 tapestry needle.

Begin with an X-wrap (see drawing on p. 17), wrapping four threads in each direction. Using the arms of the X-wrap as corner anchors, begin wrapping, following path shown in the drawing below. Wrap toward the center until the mold is covered with thread. The diagonal lines will form automatically as wrapping proceeds. Each round holds the previous round in place, and each previous round anchors the current round. End on the back and cut the thread, leaving it about 6 in. long. Thread the needle, take one stitch up through the hole in the center of the mold, over the last four wraps and down to the back. Tie off. With the tip

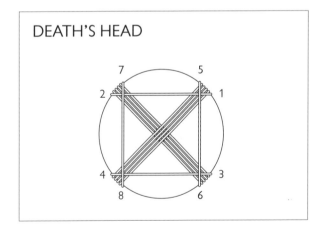

DEATH'S HEAD

Leek buttons: clockwise from upper left: star leek, death's head, checkerboard leek.

of your needle, straighten and neaten the threads on the front so that each is positioned in the order it was wrapped. None of the shanks work well on this button, so just stitch through the back of the button to attach it to your garment.

Tip: If the thread slips off the mold on the back as you near the center, break off enough thread to complete the button, thread the needle, and pass the thread under previous wraps to prevent the current wrap from slipping off.

To make a matched set of buttons, count the rounds of wrapping on the first button and use the same number on subsequent buttons. If you're not careful, and one button is even one or two rounds fuller than another, the eye will perceive that button as larger.

Star leek

CHALLENGING

Once you have mastered the death's head, you can use a needle to weave a pattern on the face of the button as wrapping proceeds. Many different patterns are possible; the star described here is just one example.

For sample in green on p. 34, you'll need:
- ⅝-in. knife-edge wood disk mold
- #16 Kanagawa silk (1000 denier)
- #24 tapestry needle.

Begin with an X-wrap of three threads each direction (see drawing on p. 17). Wrap this button the same way as the death's head. The difference in wrap-

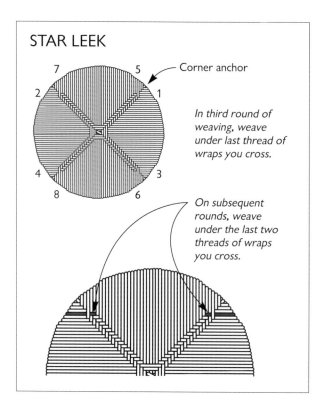

STAR LEEK

Corner anchor

In third round of weaving, weave under last thread of wraps you cross.

On subsequent rounds, weave under the last two threads of wraps you cross.

ping technique begins on the third round (drawing above): in this round, when laying down the thread from positions 1 to 2 and 3 to 4, weave it under the last thread laid down from positions 5 to 6 and 7 to 8, and vice versa. On all subsequent rounds, weave the thread under last two threads. Follow the direction for the death's head to finish.

Checkerboard leek CHALLENGING

Although you'd never guess it, this button uses the same wrapping technique as the death's head.

For samples in gray or burgundy on p. 34, you'll need:
- ¾-in. knife-edge wood disk mold
- #16 Kanagawa silk (1000 denier)
- #24 tapestry needle.

Begin with an X-wrap of four threads in each direction. Cut about 6 ft. of thread, and thread the end onto the tapestry needle. Work the same as for the death's head, but wrap six threads at each position: i.e., wrap from 1 to 2 six times, then from 3 to 4 six times, and so on (see drawing at right). When wrapping from positions 5 to 6 and 7 to 8 the second time, you must use a needle to weave over and under the previous round. To weave the pattern, go under the first six wraps at positions 1 to 2 and 3 to 4, and over the second set of six wraps at these same positions, as shown in the drawing. For the third and last round, work one set of six wraps from positions 1 to 2 going under the first set of wraps at positions 5 to 6 and 7 to 8 and over the next set. Complete the pattern with a set of six wraps going from positions 5 to 6 and working over, under, over, under, over the sets of wraps going from positions 1 to 2. Tie off on back. If the first set of

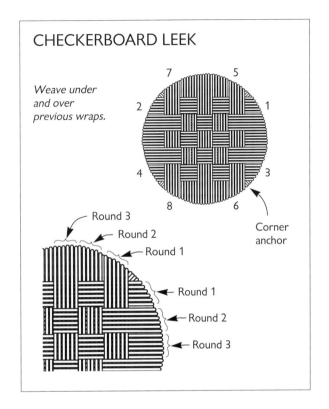

CHECKERBOARD LEEK

Weave under and over previous wraps.

wraps at 5 to 6 and 7 to 8 tends to pop off of the anchors, loop the thread around the set on the back of the button, and pull toward the center back of the mold to hold the set in place.

Teneriffe Buttons

Teneriffe lace was popularized in the early 1900s by thread manufacturers, which published instruction booklets for all types of needlework so that they could sell more thread. It is based on *sols*, or sun lace, made in Spain in the 16th and 17th centuries. The small, varied designs make beautiful buttons.

Teneriffe lace is made off the button mold and then it's mounted. The mounting method can be used for other types of lace, such as bobbin lace and tatting, where small motifs are created. I make my Teneriffe lace on a pin cushion with a paper pattern underneath. My favorite patterns are from *Teneriffe Lace* (see the Helpful Books section on p. 109). I use a photocopy machine to reduce the patterns by 80% for a size-60 mold, or 75% for a size-45 mold.

When making Teneriffe lace, be fanatical about keeping the spokes flat, in order, and untwisted. Spokes that are twisted and out of order give the lace an unkempt look.

Sun lace
MODERATE

For sample in tan at left, you'll need:
- 1⅛-in. (size-45) commercial metal button mold
- lining fabric
- 3 ft. #80 crochet cotton
- #24 tapestry needle
- 43 round-headed pins
- pin cushion.

Teneriffe and darned-net buttons: clockwise from upper left, ferris wheel, sun lace, darned net.

Cut a circle of fabric according to mold directions and baste around the outside edge. Place the mold front inside the fabric and tighten the basting thread. Tie off. Do not attach the mold back yet.

Draw a 1⅞-in. circle on a piece of paper, or photocopy the pattern to be made (see drawing below) and place it on the pin cushion. Place 42 pins—evenly spaced—around the circle with the pins at 1 and 22 being different colors or otherwise marked. Thread the needle with the crochet cotton and pin the tail out of the way opposite pin 1. Form spokes around the pins by laying the thread across the circle, to the right of pin 1, and loop it around pin 1. Cross the circle to the left of pin 22 and loop the thread around pin 22. Cross the center to the right of pin 2 and loop around it, as pin 1. Continue around all pins. Tie beginning end and long thread at center. The side you see will be the back of the lace.

Start at pin 1 and in the center to weave the pattern. Weave under two, over two threads firmly for three

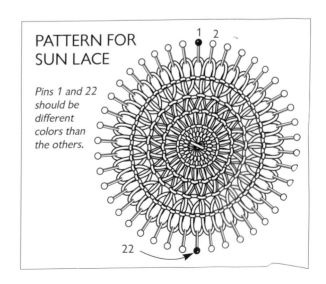

PATTERN FOR SUN LACE

Pins 1 and 22 should be different colors than the others.

1 2

22

rounds. Go over four threads at the beginning of each new row to alternate rows of weaving. Next, move the thread out ⅛ in. on a spoke and knot four threads for the round, as shown in the drawing below. Move the thread out another ⅛ in., and with two threads from one knot and two from the adjacent knot of the previous round, knot another round. Move out ⅛ in., and this time knot two threads, one each from adjacent pairs. Tie off. Remove lace from cushion. Center on button-mold front and lace across back of mold in a clock pattern. Then attach the back of the mold.

Prepare lining, form 24 spokes, and weave the first three rounds using the same techniques used on the sun-lace button on p. 39. Move out ⅛ in. and make a circle of knots, two threads to a knot. Repeat using the same two threads together. Between the two rows of knots, weave figure-eights over four threads, two threads to each leg of the figure-eight, as in the drawing below. Pass the thread from group to group along either the bottom or top row of knots (it will alternate). Move out ⅛ in. more and work a round of knots over two threads using one thread from each of two adjacent pairs. Tie off. Remove the pattern from the cushion and mount on the mold as for the sun-lace button.

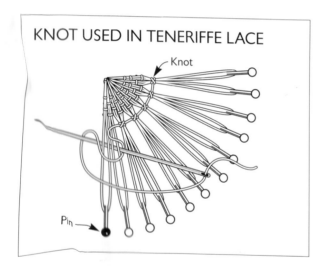

KNOT USED IN TENERIFFE LACE

Knot

Pin

Ferris wheel

MODERATE

For sample in red, gray, or blue on p. 38, you'll need:
- 1 yd. #80 crochet cotton
- 1⅛-in. (size-45) commercial metal button mold
- lining fabric
- #24 tapestry needle
- 25 round-headed pins
- pin cushion.

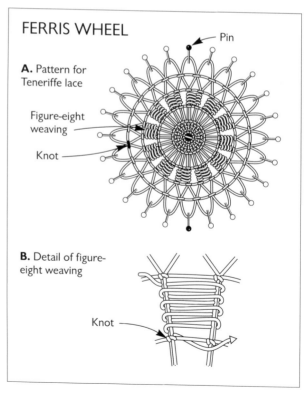

FERRIS WHEEL

Pin

A. Pattern for Teneriffe lace

Figure-eight weaving

Knot

B. Detail of figure-eight weaving

Knot

Darned-Net Buttons

Net darning is an ancient craft. Long ago, the needle-worker had to make the net before darning it, but this pattern starts with cotton tulle (also called English net), which has $1/16$-in. hexagonal spaces in its mesh. Good beginning stitches for darned net are in *McCall's Big Book of Needlecrafts* (see Helpful Books on p. 109). The nylon mold has a little more flexibility when mounting needlework and gives a little different shape.

For sample in white on green on p. 38, you'll need:
- $3/4$-in. (size-30) commercial nylon button mold
- lining fabric
- $1/16$-in. mesh cotton tulle
- #80 crochet/tatting cotton
- #26 tapestry needle.

Mark a circle on the cotton tulle sized according to the package directions on the molds for the fabric covering ($1\frac{1}{2}$ in. in this case).

Thread the tapestry needle with crochet cotton. Work a detached buttonhole stitch over one side of the hexagon in the cotton tulle, as in drawing A at right. Always point the needle toward the center of the hexagon when making detached buttonhole stitches. Work another detached buttonhole stitch on each of the other five sides of the hexagon, as shown in drawing B. After you complete the sixth detached buttonhole stitch, pass the needle down through the center of the stitched hexagon to the back of the tulle, as shown in drawing C. Come up through the center of the next hexagon in the row, skip over this hexagon and begin stitching in the next one (stitch in every other hexagon in the row). Complete enough hexagons in every other row to cover the marked circle on the tulle.

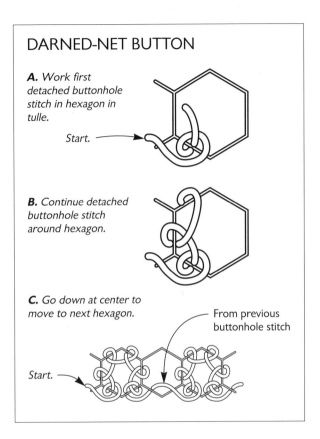

DARNED-NET BUTTON

A. Work first detached buttonhole stitch in hexagon in tulle.

Start.

B. Continue detached buttonhole stitch around hexagon.

C. Go down at center to move to next hexagon.

From previous buttonhole stitch

Start.

Cut out the circle of tulle around your stitching so that you don't cut the stitching thread. Cut a piece of lining fabric according to the package directions. Lay the tulle and lining together, and treat them as one layer. Work a running stitch around the outside of the circle. Slip the front of the button mold inside and pull up on the running stitch tightly to gather the fabric around it. Attach the back of the button according to the package directions.

Braid Buttons

Braid buttons generally fall into two groups: those buttons based on needle-lace designs and those based on sailor's knots. Braid buttons based on needle-lace designs use a mold or ring that is completely covered with braid. In general, the patterns are simplified versions or adaptations of needle-lace button patterns, but braid is used instead of thread. Braid buttons based on sailor's knots (macramé) are formed by layering or knotting the braid. No mold is used. Instead, the buttons rely on the large size and stiffness of the braid itself for support.

Braid buttons are considered to be a product of this century, although a few examples are known from the late 1800s. Before the Industrial Revolution, needle-lace buttons were wrapped with thread or cord made by a simple process of twisting several threads together. Braids were sometimes incorporated but had to be made by hand, which was very time-consuming, so braids were used only on the most expensive buttons. Along with myriad other types of machines, the Industrial Revolution brought the invention of braid-making machines, which could produce plain or fancy braids quickly and cheaply. These braids soon found their way into buttons.

Because of the large size of a braid relative to the size of the finished button, braid buttons make up quickly. Braid buttons are the only type of handmade button to survive on a commercial scale. But because they are still expensive compared with mass-produced buttons, their use is limited to evening and designer garments. For instance, Paris fashion designers have featured braid buttons from time to time; perhaps the most memorable were braid buttons on the short Chanel jackets of the 1960s. A search through some better fabric stores should uncover some commercial braid buttons that you can easily copy.

Two types of braid are commonly used for buttons: gimp and soutache. Gimp is a thin, round braid. It has one filler cord, which is wrapped with rayon in a spiral down the length of the cord. Although gimp is hard to find in single strands, it is often sold as gimp braid, which you can easily pull apart. Soutache looks like a double gimp. It has two side-by-side filler cords that are wrapped with rayon in a figure-eight pattern. Soutache braid is available in most trim departments.

But gimp and soutache are not the only braids available for button making. Many other types of small braids and cords can be used. Braid used for trim elsewhere on a garment can be made into buttons that effectively pull the design elements of the garment together. Both round and flat braids work well for buttons, and two or more different braids can be combined. For embellishment, use threads, ribbons, and beads.

When making braid buttons, it is imperative that the braid not be twisted as the button is wrapped, especially with flat braids. Even one twist in the braid will cause the button to look messy.

Ring Braid Buttons

Braid buttons made over rings have a distinctive look not duplicated in other types of buttons. The buttons draw attention because of the radiating geometrical patterns. Ring buttons are good beginning projects because they are easy to make.

Ring molds can be either plastic or rust-proof metal. Plastic rings (also called bone or café rings) used for crafts and curtains are excellent because they are lightweight and thick. Avoid thin rings because the braid does not wrap well around them. Do not use heavy (cast) metal rings because the weight of the ring causes the button to droop on the garment and might rip the garment fabric.

Many variations on the ring button are possible. Flat or round braids can be substituted for the soutache braid used in the examples in this chapter. The small hole remaining in the center of the button after the ring is wrapped can be filled with a braid knot, a braid spiral, a bead, a small button, a ribbon rose, or another suitable object.

The soutache ring buttons shown on the facing page have a hollow in the center back, leaving you with no place to attach the button to your garment, so you'll need to make a back for the button. A commercial back covered with either a shank or the thread back (see pp. 12-13) is ideal for attaching these buttons to the garment. With either back, it's important to stitch each wrap around the ring when applying the back to keep the wraps from shifting when the button is fastened through a buttonhole. I use the covered

Soutache ring buttons: clockwise from upper left, single soutache, double soutache, stacked soutache.

commercial back with thick garment fabrics because the extra height of a shank allows me to button the garment without puckering the fabric around the buttonhole. I use the thread back on lightweight garment fabrics so that the button doesn't droop.

Single soutache ring

For sample in blue on p. 45, you'll need:
- 1-in. diameter plastic ring
- 1 yd. of soutache braid
- quilting thread
- needle.

Hold the tail of the braid at the back of the plastic ring so that it sticks out away from the center (see the drawing at right). Bring the long end of the braid through the center of the ring from the back to the front. Wrap the braid over the outer edge of the ring and through the center from back to front. Working either clockwise or counterclockwise, continue wrapping the ring until it is completely covered. Push the wraps together to cover little gaps. Once the ring is wrapped, turn it over and stitch the tails to each other and to the wrap on either side with the quilting thread. Trim to 1 in. and turn the tails toward the center slightly.

To fill the center with a spiral, cut a 1½-ft. length of braid. Fold the braid at 45° ½ in. from the tail and take a stitch or two through the fold to hold it in place. This fold will hide the beginning tail of the spiral. Wrap the braid around the folded end to form a spiral. Take a stitch along the centerline of the braid through two or more layers of braid every ¼ in. or so. When the spiral is just large enough to fill the center hole of the wrapped ring, cut the braid, leaving about 1 in. Wedge the spiral into the center of the ring and tuck the beginning and ending tails toward the back. Stitch the spiral to the inside of the wrapped ring in six or eight places around the ring. Finish with either a covered commercial back or a thread back (see pp. 12-13).

If you are making a set of single soutache ring buttons, wrap them all in the same direction and count the number of wraps so that all of your buttons will look the same.

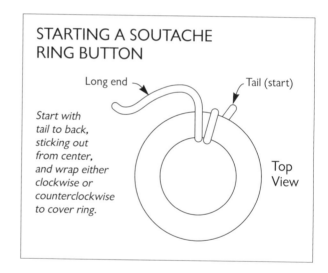

STARTING A SOUTACHE RING BUTTON

Long end

Tail (start)

Start with tail to back, sticking out from center, and wrap either clockwise or counterclockwise to cover ring.

Top View

Stacked soutache ring

The rings for stacked ring buttons are wrapped separately, then stacked, and stitched together. You might try wrapping each ring in a different color or even in a striped pattern.

For bottom samples in red on p. 45, you'll need:
- ⅝-in. diameter plastic ring
- 1-in. diameter plastic ring
- 4 ft. of soutache braid
- quilting thread
- needle.

Wrap rings individually, as you did for the single soutache ring button. To make the braid knot that will fill the center hole, take a 4-in. length of braid and form four knots so that they just touch each other. Don't pull the knots too tightly, or they will be too small and will fall through the center hole (if you make them too tight, add another knot or two). Hold the ends of the braid together so that the knots form a circle, and slip them into the center of the smaller ring, tails first. Wedge the knots down into the hole. Then thread the needle with the quilting thread and blind-stitch each knot to a wrap around the ring where the knot and wrap touch. One or two stitches per knot is sufficient. Finally, hold the large ring behind the small ring and blind-stitch the wraps of the two rings together. Use either a covered commercial back or a thread back (see pp. 12-13) to complete the button.

Double soutache ring

Double soutache ring buttons are wrapped over two rings that are glued together; stacking a smaller ring over a larger ring gives the button a domed look. Each ring is wrapped twice to give complete coverage; the first wrap forms a base for the second wrap, which can be a contrasting color.

For samples in navy and white and red and gold on p. 45, you'll need:
- ⅝-in. diameter plastic ring
- ¾-in. diameter plastic ring
- 1 yd. of soutache braid
- quilting thread
- needle
- white glue.

Glue the rings together so that the small ring fits as far down into the center of the larger ring as possible (see the drawing below). Let dry. Thread the needle with quilting thread.

Begin by holding the tail of the braid at the back of the rings so that it points away from the center, as in the drawing on the facing page. Wrap braid up through the center and down on the outside. Stitch the tail and the first wrap of braid together on the back. As you

---

MOLD OF DOUBLE SOUTACHE RING BUTTON

Side view of rings glued together

---

continue wrapping, the braid wraps will just touch on the inside of the rings. There will be gaps where the rings show on the outside. I find that 14 wraps is just right for most soutache, although you may need one more wrap or one fewer, depending on the braid. For example, metallic soutache is very stiff, so you will need at least one fewer wraps.

Wrap the braid around the rings a second time with the same or a different color so that the braid just touches on the inside—overlapping the first round—and fills the gaps on the outside. Pull the braid firmly down into the gap so that it rests on the rings. Wrap all the way around. If you want a braid knot in center, do not cut the tail. Instead, stitch the tail down where it touches the ring on the back. If you want a different center, cut the tail to 1 in. and stitch down.

For a braid knot in center, bring the braid up through the center hole. Make three loose knots that just touch each other, working each knot down to the center of the ring as it is formed. Pull the tail through the hole to the back, stopping just as the knots wedge in the hole. If your knots don't fill the hole, pull the tail back to the top and make another knot. With thread and needle, stitch the tail down securely inside the rings. Stitch each knot in place where it touches a wrap around the rings. Complete the button with a covered commercial back or a thread back.

Wrapped Braid Buttons

Wrapped braid buttons use either an X-wrap or a modified X-wrap with six or eight points. The modified X-wrap is often expanded to include many parallel wraps in each direction (sometimes as many as 15). The X-wrap itself then becomes the base covering for the button. All of the wraps in one direction are completed before beginning another wrap. You can use the method shown in the drawing below to anchor wraps as you go.

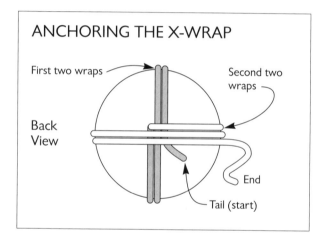

ANCHORING THE X-WRAP

First two wraps

Second two wraps

Back View

End

Tail (start)

There are two different ways of holding the braid on the mold. One method is to weave the braid through itself as the button is wrapped. The other is to use embroidery or other decorative stitches to hold the braid in place.

Wrapped braid buttons: clockwise from upper left, evening star, diamond in a square, square soutache checkerboard, silk bar, soutache checkerboard, chainette checkerboard, morning star, and in center, crossroads.

In this section I illustrate several different wrapping patterns that use the same basic method. You can easily invent other patterns, such as two-color patterns, which are attractive.

Wrapped braid buttons are bulky on the back and require you to make a self-shank, which will also secure the wraps in place. Turn the button over to the back. Pass the braid over, then under the last six wraps, as shown in the drawing below. Next, go over and catch the braid just before it passes over the six wraps. Pull snugly so that the six wraps bunch up in the center back. Now go under the diagonal wrap below the six wraps, and under the six wraps again. Wrap over and under the six wraps a second time, going in the opposite direction. Cut the tail where it emerges from under the six wraps. Although the technique described here is for a button with six wraps across the front on the last pass, it will work regardless of the number of wraps. After forming the shank, stitch it in place, and stitch the tail down. On the back, about ⅛ in. in from the edge of the button, backstitch adjacent wraps of braid together all around the button. Make sure you include the corner anchors in the stitching.

Soutache checkerboard EASY

For round sample in light blue on p. 49, you'll need:
- 1-in. diameter wood mold
- 4 ft. of soutache braid
- quilting thread
- needle
- transparent tape.

Wrap about 1 in. of transparent tape around one end of soutache braid to stiffen the end so that you can weave the pattern without a needle. Work an X-wrap over the mold, as shown in the drawing on p. 48, then come up to the front of the button after crossing the back on the diagonal. Wrap across the front of the mold just inside two arms of the X, as shown in drawing A on the facing page. Fill the space between the arms of the X with parallel wraps around the mold. It should take six wraps with soutache braid. But if you use a different braid and require more or fewer wraps, make sure you use an even number.

Cross the back of the button on the diagonal again. You'll be at the same anchor where you began the first wrap but on the other side of it. Begin wrapping at right angles to the first six wraps. For the first three wraps (or half of the number you made the first time,

---

MAKING A SELF-SHANK

1. Pass braid over then under last six wraps.

2. Pull braid snug. Go under diagonal wrap and last six wraps again.

3. Pass over six wraps, then under once more, going in the opposite direction. Cut braid where it emerges, then stitch down.

Back View

SOUTACHE CHECKERBOARD BUTTON

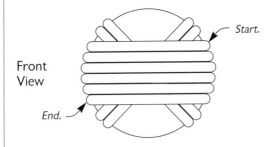

Front View

Start.

End.

A. *Make first six wraps of braid between arms of X.*

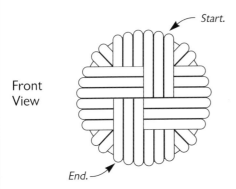

Front View

Start.

End.

B. *Weave second six wraps at 90° to first six. For first three wraps, go over three, then under three, and alternate on last three wraps.*

which explains why you need an even number), go over the first three wraps of the first round and under the last three, as shown in drawing B at left. On the next three wraps, go under the first three wraps of the first round and over the last three. Complete the back of the button by making a self-shank.

Chainette checkerboard   EASY

For sample in cranberry on p. 49, you'll need:

- 1-in. diameter wood mold
- 8 ft. of chainette braid
- quilting thread
- needle
- transparent tape.

Follow the directions for the soutache checkerboard, but for the chainette checkerboard, make approximately 14 parallel wraps in each direction. The number of wraps will depend on the size of your chainette braid. The rule of thumb is to use enough wraps to cover the mold, but be sure to use an even number of wraps so that you can divide the first wraps evenly when you weave the second set of wraps.

Because chainette is a thinner, more flexible braid than soutache, you could use a covered commercial back and thus eliminate making a self-shank.

Square soutache checkerboard

For sample in light blue on p. 49, you'll need:
- ⅝-in. square cut from mat board
- 1 yd. of soutache braid
- quilting thread
- needle
- transparent tape.

This square button uses the same technique as the round checkerboard button. Corner anchors aren't necessary because the edge of the button is square, and the braid doesn't slip off the mold as it does on a round edge. To prevent show-through, use a permanent marker to color the corners of the mat board to match your braid.

Crossroads EASY

For sample in red on p. 49, you'll need:
- 1-in. diameter wood mold
- 4 ft. of soutache braid
- quilting thread
- needle
- transparent tape.

This button is worked the same as the checkerboard soutache button, except for the weaving pattern. Work the X-wrap and first six wraps the same way you would work them for the checkerboard soutache button. Cross the back on the diagonal and come up on the opposite side. Make three wraps as shown in

drawing A below. While making the final three wraps, weave in and out of the previous three, as shown in drawing B. Complete the back of the button with a self-shank and anchor the wraps with backstitches (see drawing on p. 50).

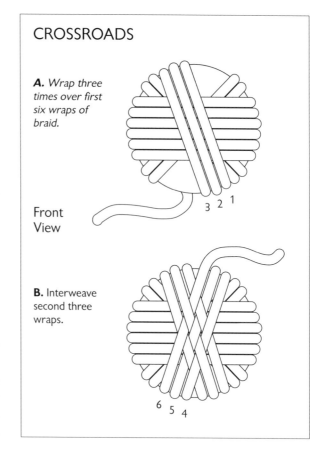

CROSSROADS

A. *Wrap three times over first six wraps of braid.*

Front View

B. Interweave second three wraps.

Diamond in a square   EASY

For sample in yellow on p. 49, you'll need:

- 1-in. diameter wood mold
- 4 ft. of soutache braid
- quilting thread
- needle
- transparent tape.

This button is another variation of the checkerboard soutache button. Work the X-wrap and first six wraps the same as for the checkerboard. The weaving pattern is worked at 90° to the first six wraps, so begin by crossing the back on the diagonal and coming up on the opposite side. The first wrap is woven under the first and over the last five wraps, as shown in the drawing below. The next four wraps are woven under the first wrap, over the middle four wraps, and under

WEAVING PATTERN FOR
DIAMOND IN A SQUARE

1 2 3 4 5 6

Second round
of wraps

Front
View

First round
of wraps

the last wrap. The last wrap is woven over the first five and under the last wrap. Finish the back of the button (see drawing on p. 50) before weaving the diamond pattern on the top.

The diamond is made with a separate 6-in. length of braid taped at one end. On the front, pass the braid under the top six wraps, pulling it through just enough so that the tail is hidden. Weave the braid diagonally under, then over each of the four sides of the square. To finish, pass the braid back under the top wraps in the opposite direction of the original tail. Cut the tail off so that it is hidden under the wraps, and stitch or glue the tails in place.

Morning star   MODERATE

Gimp seems to vary a lot in size. When making a button, adjust the number of base wraps so that the gimp covers the mold nicely in the finished button.

For sample in lavender on p. 49, you'll need:

- 1-in. diameter flat wood mold
- 3 yd. of gimp
- #18 tapestry needle.

Begin covering the mold by wrapping the gimp around the mold seven times, working to the right and catching the tail as you wrap (see drawing A on. p. 54). Rotate the button 90° clockwise and repeat the wrapping pattern. Rotate the button 45°, wrap seven times, then rotate 90° from that round of wraps, and repeat. This button will require a total of four rounds of seven base wraps.

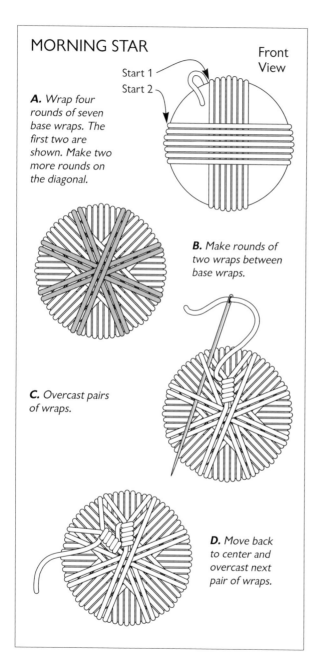

MORNING STAR

Front View

Start 1

Start 2

A. Wrap four rounds of seven base wraps. The first two are shown. Make two more rounds on the diagonal.

B. Make rounds of two wraps between base wraps.

C. Overcast pairs of wraps.

D. Move back to center and overcast next pair of wraps.

Next, make two wraps of gimp across the center between two rounds of seven, as in drawing B at left. Repeat wraps four times around the button.

Thread the tapestry needle onto the gimp. From the back, pass the needle and gimp through the hole in the center of the mold to the front. Take one strand of gimp from each of two adjacent wraps in drawing B and overcast them together five times each (see drawing C), working from the center out. Keep the overcast stitches as close to the center as possible. Move back to the center of the button and repeat (drawing D). Continue around the button until all pairs are wrapped. Pass the needle and gimp to the back through the hole in the mold and tie off by overcasting about six gimp cords two or three times at center back. Pass the gimp 1 in. under the base wraps and cut. To attach the button to your garment, simply sew through the gimp on the back of the button.

Evening star

MODERATE

For sample in champagne on p. 49, you'll need:
- 1-in. diameter flat wood mold
- 3 yd. of gimp
- quilting thread
- #18 tapestry needle
- sharp needle.

This button is covered with a base of four rounds of five wraps each. Hold the tail at the center back of the mold. Wrap gimp around the mold five times, working from left to right. Rotate the button 90° clockwise and make five more wraps, again working to the right (see drawing A on the facing page). Rotate the button 45°, make five more wraps, and then rotate the button 90° and make five more wraps.

EVENING STAR

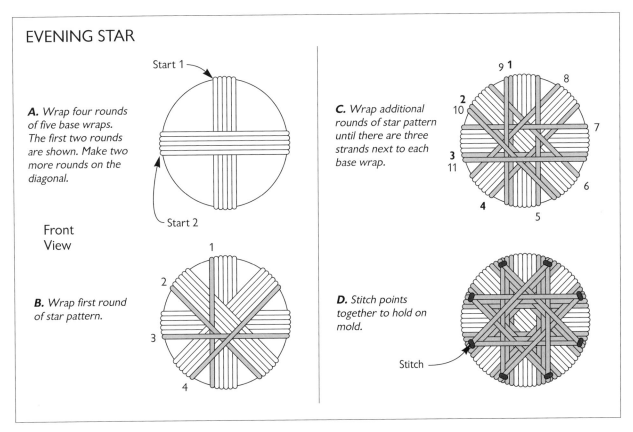

A. Wrap four rounds of five base wraps. The first two rounds are shown. Make two more rounds on the diagonal.

Start 1

Start 2

Front View

B. Wrap first round of star pattern.

C. Wrap additional rounds of star pattern until there are three strands next to each base wrap.

D. Stitch points together to hold on mold.

Stitch

Now begin the star pattern by wrapping a single strand of gimp to the left of the round of wraps located in the 12 o'clock to 6 o'clock position. Turn the button clockwise, so the next round of five wraps is in the 12 o'clock to 6 o'clock position, and wrap one strand of gimp to the left of this round, as shown in drawing B. Continue turning and wrapping—always to the left—until there are three strands of gimp on each side of each round of five wraps (see drawing C).

Thread the tapestry needle onto the gimp. Make two or three parallel stitches over about six strands of gimp near the center back to form a shank. Pass the gimp 1 in. under the base wraps and cut.

Secure the points of the star so that they don't slide off the mold. Thread quilting thread onto a sharp needle. On the front of the button, where the last two strands of gimp cross to form a star point, stitch the two strands together (see drawing D). Pass the needle and thread under the gimp on top of the button to the next point. Continue stitching points around the button. Tie the thread off on the back. To attach the button to the garment, sew through the shank.

Silk bar

MODERATE

For sample in gold on p. 49, you'll need:
- ⅝-in. diameter wood mold
- #16 Kanagawa silk (1000 denier)
- #26 tapestry needle.

For this button, eight rounds of six wraps serve as both the base wraps and the spokes. To begin, hold the thread tail at center back. Wrap thread around the mold six times, working left to right. Rotate the button 90° clockwise and repeat. Rotate the button 45° and then 90°, making six more wraps in each position. Now go back and fill in the gaps between these rounds with six more wraps in each gap.

To make the top design, cut the thread to about 2 ft. Thread the needle on the silk and pass the needle from back to front through the hole in the center of the mold. Overcast each round of six wraps on the top layer four times, working from the center toward the outside, as in drawing C on p. 54. Do not pull the overcast stitches tight; leave them loose enough so that the wraps don't gather together. Work eight sets of overcast stitches around the button. Pass the needle to the back through the center hole and tie off. To attach the button to the garment, sew through the gimp on the back of the button and then through your garment fabric.

Knotted Buttons

Many beautiful knotted buttons were made out of rope by sailors on long sea voyages. The buttons were used to decorate rope-covered picture frames and other remembrances to be given to loved ones back home. The book *Encyclopedia of Knots and Fancy Rope Work* (see Helpful Books on p. 109) shows how to form many knots that can be used as buttons.

Knotted buttons can be used with regular buttonholes, but they are particularly appropriate when used with frogs, which are decorative buttonhole closures (see Chapter 5). The button can be worked directly into the braid or cord used to make the frog, becoming an integral part of the frog. There is no chance of the button ever coming loose or falling off.

Ball

MODERATE

For upper-right sample in metallic gold on the facing page, you'll need:
- 1 yd. of braid
- thread
- needle
- transparent tape.

The weaving of this knot can be confusing until you master the in-and-out sequence. You may want to photocopy the drawing on p. 58, place it on top of a piece

Knotted buttons: clockwise from upper left, toggle, ball, Turk's head, monkey's fist.

of cardboard or foam board, and then pin the braid on top of the photocopy when learning.

Tape one end of the braid to make weaving the knot easier. Following the drawing at right: make loop 1 first, then lap loop 2 over loop 1. When you get to loop 3, start weaving in and out of loops 1 and 2. When forming an odd-numbered loop (i.e., loop 3), weave over the sides of even-numbered loops and under the sides of other odd-numbered loops; for an even-numbered loop (i.e., loop 4), weave over the sides of odd-numbered loops and under the sides of other even-numbered loops. Form a second round of loops inside the outer round by exactly tracing the route of the outer round of braid.

Pull loops tight, starting with the outside round and working toward center. Tighten each loop in order: loop 1, then loop 2, and so on. The outer loops pull toward the back of the button to form a ball. The knot must be pulled very tight, or it will stretch out of shape when used. I pull the knot tight in two passes, which gives me a more even ball. Cut the tails close to the back. Sew through the back of the button to attach it to your garment.

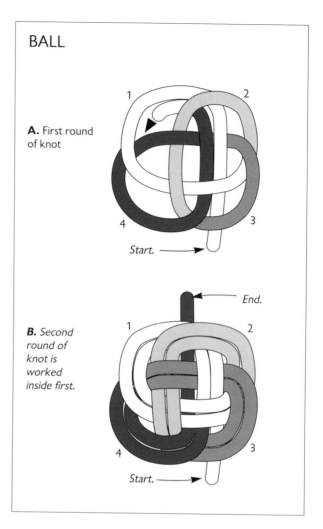

BALL

A. First round of knot

B. Second round of knot is worked inside first.

Toggle

The toggle is a wonderfully easy-to-make button. Simply wrap the braid around your finger (or a dowel) three, four, five, or more times, depending on the length of toggle you want.

For upper-left sample in metallic gold on p. 57, you'll need:
- 1 ft. of braid.

Lay the braid along your finger (or a dowel), with the short tail toward your palm, as shown in the drawing at right. With the long end, wrap loosely back over the short tail and your finger five times, moving from fingertip toward palm. Gently remove the wraps from your finger, holding them all in order. Thread the long tail back through the center. Pull on each tail and twist the wraps tightly until the knot is hard. The knot must be very tight, or it will stretch out of shape with use. Cut the tails close to the knot. The tails are caught inside the knot, so no sewing is necessary to keep the tails neat.

TOGGLE

A. Lay braid along finger or a dowel.

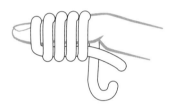

B. Wrap braid over finger and beginning tail five times.

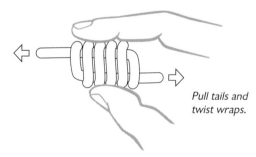

Pull tails and twist wraps.

C. Remove finger, tuck ending tail through center of wraps, pull tails, and twist wraps.

Monkey's fist

The monkey's-fist knot will be familiar to anyone who has done macramé. The bead in the center dictates the size of the finished button; its role as a mold is secondary. You'll have to experiment with the size of the bead, the diameter of braid, and the number or wraps in each direction to get the size button you want. The wraps should just cover the bead.

For sample in red on p. 57, you'll need:
- ¾-in. round bead
- 1½ yd. of ⅛-in. diameter braid.

Start this knot over your fingers. Wrap the braid around your forefinger and middle finger four times, as shown in drawing A (right). Then wrap around your middle finger once. Working from back to front and from bottom to top, wrap the braid around the center of the first four wraps four times. Pass the braid through the four loops at the top formed by the first four wraps (drawing B). Gently remove your fingers, keeping all wraps in order, and insert the bead into the center of the wraps. Wrap four times through the lower loops and then through the upper loops formed by the first four wraps (drawing C). Tighten the braid around the bead by pulling each wrap in the order it was laid down. Cut the ends close. Apply a drop of glue inside to hold the ends in place.

MONKEY'S FIST

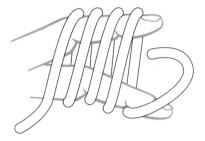

A. *Wrap braid over fingers four times.*

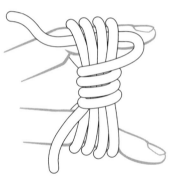

B. *Wrap braid around center four times and pass last wrap through upper group of loops.*

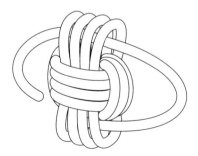

C. *Insert bead and make four wraps.*

Turk's head

The Turk's head is couched onto a mold that is covered with matching fabric to create a button. Couching uses tiny stitches to hold braid onto the mold. To hide the stitches, use a matching color thread and position stitches in a groove or a twist or at the back of the braid.

For bottom-right sample in metallic gold on p. 57, you'll need:
- ¾-in. (size 30) commercial button mold covered with fabric to match braid
- 1 yd. of braid
- thread
- needle.

As you form this knot, you will make six interwoven loops on the first pass. If you find it too confusing, photocopy the figure, place it on top of a piece of cardboard or foam board, and then pin the braid on top of the photocopy while forming the knot.

Tape one end of the braid to make weaving easier. Following the drawing at right, form the outer round of the Turk's-head knot. When you get to loop 4, start weaving in and out of loops 1, 2, and 3. Loops 5 and 6 are also woven through previous loops. Form a second round of loops inside the outer round by tracing the route of the outer round of braid. Adjust the tightness of the loops, starting with loop 1 on the outer round and working in the same order that the loops were formed. Make the knot slightly larger than the covered mold. With needle and thread, stitch the knot to the fabric on the button mold.

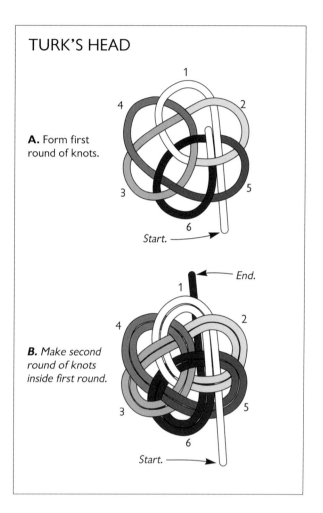

TURK'S HEAD

A. Form first round of knots.

Start.

End.

B. Make second round of knots inside first round.

Start.

Crocheted Buttons

Crocheted buttons were used extensively from 1860 until 1920. Shirtwaists and dresses of the 1860s were often decorated with crocheted buttons in long, closely spaced rows down the front and sleeves. Tiny crocheted ball buttons in black or colors were among the most stylish. Most of these crocheted buttons were produced in cottage industries supporting the Paris fashion industry.

The invasion of Paris in 1870 during the Franco-Prussian War temporarily ended production of crocheted buttons. By 1880 production was in full swing again, but the style of crocheted buttons had changed. Large black, elaborately designed buttons became popular; the fancier versions incorporated bullions and beads. Black buttons were used on garments of all colors probably in part because black did not show the dirt in a time when better garments were only spot-cleaned. But more important, it was a time when rigid mourning customs were followed, especially in the United States and England. Queen Victoria, for example, wore black for the last 20 years of her reign to mourn the death of Prince Albert.

Another revival of crocheted buttons occurred during the Edwardian period, from 1901 to 1910. The buttons of this period were usually white and of simpler design than Victorian-era buttons, although they often still incorporated bullions. Like shirtwaist buttons, crocheted buttons complemented the lace-encrusted waists and Irish crochet of the period.

Crocheted buttons make up quickly and easily: Each of the buttons in this chapter can be made in 45 minutes or less. Crochet motifs, worked like miniature doilies, are mounted on molds to make crocheted buttons. The technique is no different from other crochet, but the scale is considerably smaller. Some of these buttons require no more knowledge of crochet than the single crochet stitch.

In general, crocheted buttons are made using steel crochet hooks and fine threads. Working with a steel hook and fine thread is not difficult because all of the stitches are the same as in crochet with yarn. But you want to work tightly; otherwise, the crochet will be flimsy and lose its durability.

Crochet motifs easily adapt to different threads, hook sizes, or individual tension with only slight modifications to the patterns given here. If a test button doesn't make up in exactly the right size, try using a different mold size, thread size, hook, or add or delete a round of crochet.

Even when fine threads are used, the crochet has substantial thickness. It can add as much as ⅛ in. to the diameter of a mold. It is too thick to be caught in the back of a commercial mold so, like the mounting method used on old crocheted buttons, it forms a cap over the mold. If you make the button over a commercial mold, cover the mold with fabric that matches the crochet you choose.

Abbreviations and Symbols

The following abbreviations and symbols are used in the crochet instructions in this chapter. British terms, where they are different, are given in parentheses.

bet	between
ch	chain
dc	double crochet (treble crochet)
hdc	half double crochet (half treble crochet)
lp	loop
rnd	round
sc	single crochet (double crochet)
sk	skip
sl st	slip stitch (single crochet)
st(s)	stitch(es)
tc	triple crochet
tog	together
yo	yarn over
[ ]	work the number of times stated; example: [ch 5, sc] 5 times
* *	the sequence between asterisks is repeated as many times as necessary to reach the end of the row; example: *2sc in each sc* around.

The crochet motif is held on the mold by two rounds of decrease (one stitch in every other stitch of the previous round). Because you hold the mold against the back of the crochet while working the decreases, the crochet will collapse toward the center back of the mold, thereby capturing the mold.

The buttons in this chapter are arranged in order of difficulty. The first two buttons are based on the single-crochet stitch. The following buttons use increasingly difficult stitches and introduce techniques such as crocheting over a ring. If you are just learning how to crochet or are not comfortable crocheting with thread, select a button near the beginning of this chapter.

The abbreviations and symbols shown on the facing page are used in the crochet instructions for each button. (Also see the chart below for more information about hooks.) For more detailed information on how to crochet, refer to *The Harmony Guide to Crochet Stitches* (see Helpful Books on p. 109) or another crochet reference book.

Steel Crochet Hook Sizes														
largest													smallest	
U.S.	1	2	3	4	5	6	7	8	9	10	11	12	13	14
U.K.	3/0	2/0	1/0	1	1½	2	2½	3	4	5	5½	6	6½	7
Continental (mm)	3	2.5		2		1.75	1.5	1.25	1	.75		.6		

Steel crochet hooks have standardized sizes, but sizing and numbering systems may differ, depending on the country of origin. U.S. steel crochet hook numbers get larger as the hook gets smaller. U.K. numbers work the same way. Continental steel sizes work the opposite: As the hook sizes get smaller, so do the numbers.

Circular Crochet Buttons

Most commonly used on Edwardian-period clothing, circular crochet buttons were usually white and were made of cotton thread in sizes comparable to sizes 80 to 5 crochet cotton. Silk threads were not used because they would not have withstood the boiling and bleaching to which these buttons were subjected when garments were washed.

Circular crochet buttons are the simplest crocheted buttons to make. Nearly any thread or small cord can be used, and the button can be made in any size. Circle and spiral buttons are made in a similar manner, except rounds for the circle are joined, and rounds for the spiral are not.

Circle

EASY

For sample in metallic gold on the facing page, you'll need:

- 1-in. (size 45) commercial half-round button mold covered with gold lamé fabric
- Gold Rush XS, Candlelight gold, or similar metallic yarn
- #9 steel crochet hook (U.K. #4, see chart on p. 65).

SLIP STITCH

The slip stitch is used to join a round of crochet. Insert hook into top of first stitch of round. Wrap thread over hook. Pull thread through both loops on hook.

Rnd 1: ch 4, sl st to form ring (see drawing at right on p. 68).

Rnd 2: ch 2, 7 sc in ring. Join (see drawing at left on p. 68 and drawing above).

Rnd 3: ch 2 (counts as first sc). *2 sc in each sc* around. Join. (16 stitches)

Rnds 4, 5: ch 2 (counts as first sc). *2 sc in first and 1 sc in next sc* around. Join. (24, 36 stitches)

Rnds 6, 7: ch 2 (counts as first sc). *sc* around. Join. Insert mold after rnd 7.

Rnds 8, 9: ch 1, *sc in every other st* around. Tie off.

Circular crocheted buttons: clockwise from left, circle, pearl, spiral.

SINGLE CROCHET STITCH

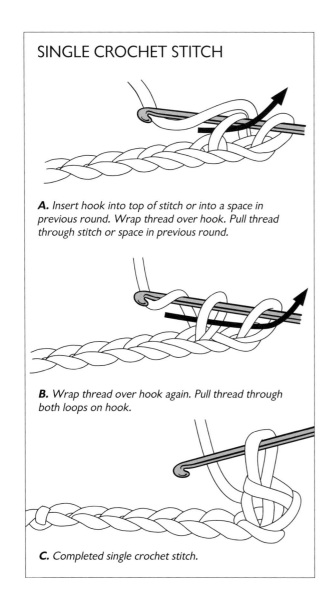

A. Insert hook into top of stitch or into a space in previous round. Wrap thread over hook. Pull thread through stitch or space in previous round.

B. Wrap thread over hook again. Pull thread through both loops on hook.

C. Completed single crochet stitch.

CHAIN START

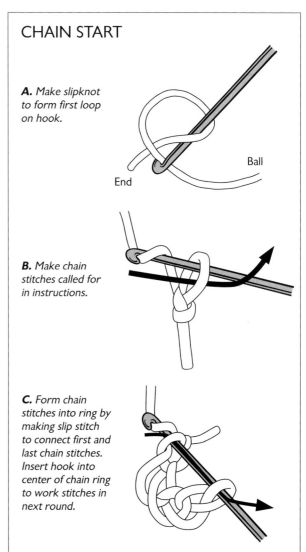

A. Make slipknot to form first loop on hook.

Ball

End

B. Make chain stitches called for in instructions.

C. Form chain stitches into ring by making slip stitch to connect first and last chain stitches. Insert hook into center of chain ring to work stitches in next round.

Spiral

The same simple method used to make the circle button can be used to make a button with a spiral look. Just eliminate the join at the end of each round.

For sample in white on p. 67, you'll need:
- ⁷⁄₁₆-in. (size 18) commercial flat button mold covered with fabric
- silk buttonhole twist, size D (30 or 30/3)
- #14 steel crochet hook (U.K. #7).

Rnd 1: In loop start (see drawing below), make 6 sc. Pull tail to tighten center.

Rnds 2, 3: *2 sc in each sc* around. Do not join. (12, 24 stitches)

Rnd 4: *sc in first sc, 2 sc in next sc* around. (36 stitches)

Rnds 5, 6, 7: *sc* around. Weave beginning tail into back of work. Insert mold after rnd 7.

Rnds 8, 9: *sc in every other sc* around. Tie off.

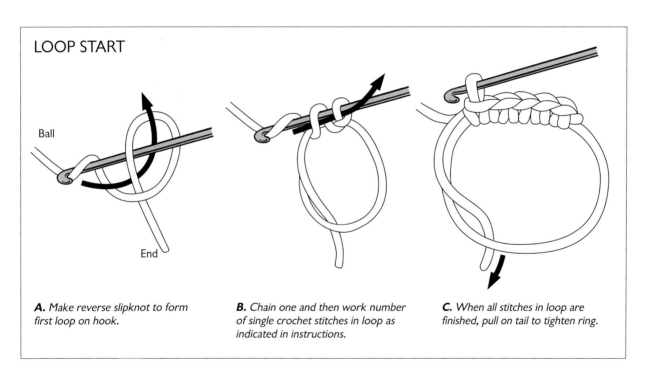

LOOP START

Ball

End

A. *Make reverse slipknot to form first loop on hook.*

B. *Chain one and then work number of single crochet stitches in loop as indicated in instructions.*

C. *When all stitches in loop are finished, pull on tail to tighten ring.*

Pearl

Early this century, Parisian prostitutes hung pearl buttons from their clothing so that the movement attracted attention as they walked. No respectable Parisian woman would have used them on her clothing! Today, however, a row of closely spaced pearl buttons in rayon or silk makes a lovely closure for a wedding gown or party dress.

For bottom-right sample in white on p. 67, you'll need:
- 10 mm wood bead or stuffed mold
- silk buttonhole twist, size D (30 or 30/3)
- #14 steel crochet hook.

Rnd 1: In loop start (see drawing on p. 69), make 5 sc. sl st to join. Pull tail to tighten center.
Rnd 2: ch 2 (counts as first sc). *2 sc in each sc* around. Do not join. (10 stitches)
Rnds 3, 4, 5: *1 sc in first and second sc, 2 sc in third sc* around. Weave beginning tail into inside of work. (13, 17, 23 stitches)
Rnds 6, 7, 8, 9: *sc* around. (23 stitches each)
Rnd 10: *sc in first and second sc, sk next sc* around. Insert mold.
Rnd 11: *sc in first and second sc, sk next sc* until all stitches are used.
Shank: ch 3, sl st in first ch. Tie off.

Cluster Buttons

There are many different cluster-, puff-, and popcorn-type stitches that can be used to create buttons. For larger buttons, you can either use a larger hook, thread, and mold or add more rounds of cluster stitch.

Cluster

For sample in ecru at right, you'll need:
- $^9/_{16}$-in. (size 24) commercial half-round button mold covered with fabric
- #80 crochet cotton
- #14 steel crochet hook (U.K. #7).

Cluster stitch: dc5tog (see drawing on p. 72)
Rnd 1: ch 8. Join with sl st.
Rnd 2: ch 2 (counts as first dc). [dc5tog, ch 2] 8 times in circle. sl st to join in top of first cluster.
Rnd 3: sl st into ch 2 lp. ch 2 (counts as first dc). *[dc5tog, ch 2] 2 times in each ch 2 lp* around. sl st to join in top of first cluster.
Rnd 4: sl st into ch 2 lp. ch 2 (counts as first dc). *3 dc in ch 2 lp* around. Join. Insert mold.
Rnds 5, 6: *sc in every other st* around. Tie off.

Cluster, loop, and ring crocheted buttons: clockwise from left, Irish rose, floribunda arch, cluster.

CLUSTER STITCH

A. *Over chain stitches of previous round, make five double crochet stitches, leaving last loop of each double crochet on hook.*

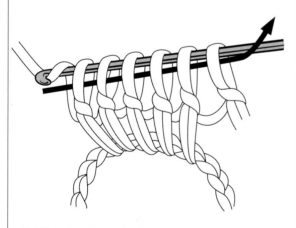

B. *Wrap thread over hook and pull through all loops on hook.*

Loop Buttons

Irish rose was one of the most elaborate of the Edwardian crocheted buttons. Most buttons in this style appear to have been made by a seamstress or a woman at home, following patterns published in women's magazines of the time. Instructions for an Irish-rose button and several other similar ones were printed in the April 1903 issue of *Delineator*, a fashion magazine that included paper patterns in each issue.

One feature of Irish crochet that's used in buttons is multiple layers of crochet. The rose petals are formed by working stitches with increasing height to the center of the petal and then working mirror-image, decreasing-height stitches. A loop is formed behind one petal over which the petal of the next round is worked.

Irish rose

MODERATE

For samples in blue on p. 71, you'll need:
- 7/8-in. (size 36) commercial half-round button mold covered with fabric
- #80 crochet cotton
- #14 steel crochet hook (U.K. #7).

Rnd 1: ch 8, sl st to form ring.

Rnd 2: ch 5. [dc, ch 2] 7 times in ring. sl st in third lp of ch 5 to join. (8 loops) (see drawing on p. 74)

Rnd 3: ch 1 (counts as first sc). *[sc, 5 dc, sc] over ch 2* around.

Rnd 4: Without turning work, *ch 3 on back, sl st bet 2 petals* around. (8 loops)

Rnd 5: sl st into lp. ch 1 (counts as first sc). *[sc, 7 dc, sc] over ch 3 lp* around. Join.

Rnd 6: *ch 4, sl st bet 2 petals* around. (8 loops)

Rnd 7: sl st into lp. ch 1 (counts as first sc). *[sc, hdc, 9 dc, hdc, sc] over ch 4 lp* around. Join. (see drawing at right)

Rnd 8: *ch 5, sl st bet 2 petals* around. (8 loops)

Rnd 9: sl st into first lp. ch 2 (counts as first dc). *7 dc in each lp* around. Join.

Rnd 10: ch 2 (counts as first dc). *dc* around. Join. Insert mold.

Rnds 11, 12: *sc in every other st* around. Tie off.

HALF DOUBLE CROCHET

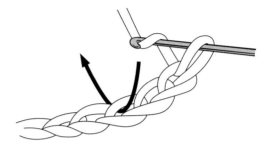

A. *Wrap thread over hook and insert hook into top of stitch or loop in previous round.*

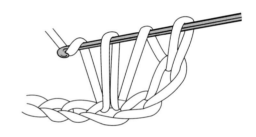

B. *Wrap thread over hook and pull hook through stitch or loop in previous row. Wrap thread over hook again.*

C. *Pull hook through all loops on hook.*

DOUBLE CROCHET

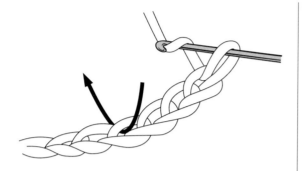

A. Wrap thread over hook and insert hook into top of stitch or through loop in previous round.

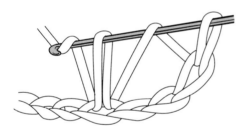

B. Wrap thread over hook and pull hook through stitch or loop in previous row. Wrap thread over hook again.

C. Pull hook through first two loops on hook. Wrap thread over hook.

D. Pull hook through all loops on hook.

Ring Buttons

The late Victorian-era black crocheted buttons nearly always incorporated metal rings, which stabilized portions of the pattern on the button mold so that the design remained recognizable. Many different ring shapes were used. Round rings in many sizes were the most common, but square, oval, diamond, and heart-shaped rings were also used. Multiple rings were featured in some of the more elaborate buttons.

The metal rings were covered with single crochet stitches, as shown in the drawing below. Sometimes the same single crochet stitches also caught loops or bullion stitches from previous rounds to hold them in place. The overall look is very formal.

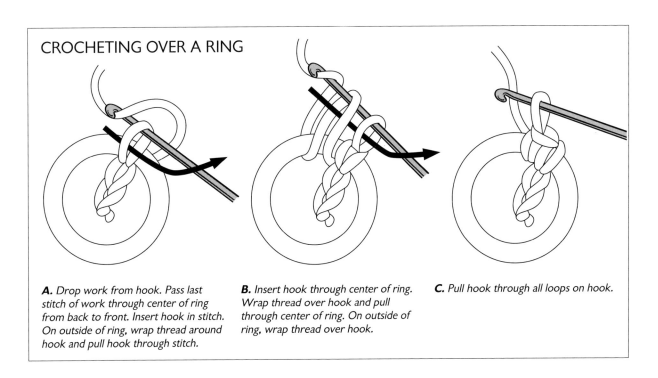

CROCHETING OVER A RING

A. Drop work from hook. Pass last stitch of work through center of ring from back to front. Insert hook in stitch. On outside of ring, wrap thread around hook and pull hook through stitch.

B. Insert hook through center of ring. Wrap thread over hook and pull through center of ring. On outside of ring, wrap thread over hook.

C. Pull hook through all loops on hook.

Floribunda arch

For sample in gold on p. 71, you'll need:
- ½-in. brass ring
- ⅞-in. (size 36) commercial half-round button mold covered with fabric
- #80 crochet cotton
- #14 steel crochet hook (U.K. #7).

Rnd 1: [ch 6, sl st in slipknot] 4 times, ch 3, tc in first ch of ch 6.
Rnd 2: Drop thread from hook. Hold crochet in ring so that lp of crochet is in front of ring and ball thread is behind ring. Pick up lp with crochet hook and sl st around ring. [10 sc around ring, sc through ch 6 and around ring together] 4 times, 11 sc over ring. Join.
Rnd 3: *ch 5, skip 6 st, sc in 7th st* around. (8 loops)
Rnd 4: *8 sc over ch 5 lp* around.
Rnds 5-9: *sc* around. Insert mold after rnd 9.
Rnds 10, 11: *sc in every other st* around. Tie off.

Bullion Buttons

The bullion stitch (see the drawing on p. 78) was the hallmark of black crocheted buttons. The bullions were formed over a tiny ring and often had a larger ring around the outer edge of the group. Bullions were made using a special crochet hook with a shank that was exactly the size of the hook and did not taper. This hook made bullions that were of consistent diameter over their length. But bullion crochet hooks are no longer made. To make firm, tight bullions using modern hooks, choose one with a shank no larger than the hook and no taper to the shank. Of the modern hooks, I prefer Susan Bates Steelite hooks.

Tiny rings for the center of the bullions are hard to find. A model shop may have tiny steel washers that can be used, but I find it more convenient to make my own center rings from a soft-drink bottle. To make a ring, cut out a ¼-in. diameter circle from the plastic with a paper punch. Then, in the center of this circle, punch a ⅛-in. hole (¼- and ⅛-in. paper punches are available at any office-supply store).

Bullion crocheted buttons: clockwise from upper left, stacked bullion, concentric ring, baby bullions.

BULLION STITCH

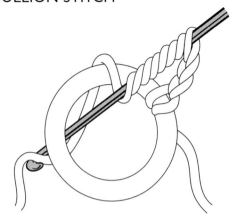

Wrap thread over hook seven times (or as many times as indicated in instructions). Insert hook in center of ring or through stitch of previous round. Holding the seven loops of thread on shank of hook with your thumb and index finger, pull hook through all loops on shank. If hook won't slide through loops, wrap loops a little more loosely. Chain 1 at top of bullion to lock stitch in place.

Baby bullion

For samples in gray on p. 77, you'll need:
- ¼-in. plastic bullion ring
- ⁹⁄₁₆-in. (size 24) commercial half-round button mold covered with fabric
- buttonhole twist
- #13 steel crochet hook (U.K. #6.5).

Rnd 1: Attach thread to ring. [yo 8 bullion, sc over ring] 10 times. Join where thread was attached to ring.
Rnd 2: ch 1. *2 sc in top of each bullion* around. (20 stitches)
Rnds 3, 4: *sc* around. Insert mold after rnd 4.
Rnds 5, 6: *sc in every other st* around. Tie off.

Stacked bullion CHALLENGING

For sample in blue on p. 77. you'll need:

- ¼-in. plastic bullion ring
- 1¼-in. (size 60) commercial half-round button mold covered with fabric
- #12 pearl cotton
- #12 steel crochet hook (U.K. #6).

Rnd 1: Attach thread to ring. ch 1. [yo 10 bullion, sc over ring] 6 times. sl st in top of bullion to join.

Rnd 2: ch 1. *2 yo 10 bullions in bullion, ch 5* around. sl st in bullion to join.

Rnd 3: sl st bet bullions. ch 1. *ch 1, 2 yo 10 bullions bet bullion pair, ch 1, 8 sc over ch 5* around. Join.

Rnd 4: sl st bet bullions. ch 1. *ch 1, 1 yo 10 bullion bet bullion pair, ch 1, sc in each sc* around. Join.

Rnds 5-8: *sc* around. Insert mold after rnd 8.

Rnds 9, 10: *sc in every other st* around. Tie off.

Concentric rings CHALLENGING

For sample in rose on p. 77, you'll need:

- ¼-in. plastic bullion ring
- 9/16-in. brass ring
- 1¼-in. (size 60) commercial half-round button mold covered with fabric
- #12 pearl cotton
- #12 steel crochet hook (U.K. #6).

Rnd 1: Attach thread to ring. ch 2. [yo 10 bullion] 12 times. sl st in top of bullion to join.

Rnd 2: Drop thread from hook. Place crochet center inside brass ring with ball thread to back of ring and lp to front. Pick up lp. ch 1, *yo 10 bullion in bullion, 3 sc over ring* around. Join.

Rnd 3: *ch 5, sc in bullion* around. Join.

Rnd 4: *7 sc in ch 5 lp* around. Do not join.

Rnds 5-8: *sc* around. Insert mold after rnd 8.

Rnds 9, 10: *sc in every other st* around. Tie off.

Frog Closures

A frog is a decorative button closure formed from a loop of braid, cord, or fabric, and then appliquéd onto the garment. The button is often worked directly into the braid, becoming an integral part of the closure. The size and decorative nature of a frog closure make it a major design element of the garment on which it is used. Ethnic clothing often features beautiful frogs, which serve practical purposes.

Frogs eliminate the need to cut the fabric to make buttonholes, so more of the fabric is kept intact, and valuable wools and silks can be recut and used for other garments. Frogs also make it easier to work with fabrics that ravel easily when cut, such as hand-woven wool, which is often used in traditional garments from northern Europe and Asia.

Frogs are made in either one- or two-piece versions. Each half of the two-piece frog is appliquéd to a side of the opening; one half has a loop for a buttonhole, and the other has a button sewn onto the loop. A one-piece frog, traditionally used on asymmetrical openings, has a decorative loop on the buttonhole side and uses a regular button on the other. However, a one-piece frog designed with a loop on both sides also works well on a centered opening, with each loop fitting over its own button.

All kinds of commercial buttons work with frog closures, and many of the buttons in this book will work, as well. Knotted braid buttons (see pp. 56-61) and beads are the most traditional buttons used with frog closures. But be creative: A variety of objects can be sewn or tied onto a garment. I once saw a twig used for a button with a free-form frog.

The frogs in this chapter can be made with a variety of braids, cords, or fabrics. The stiffness of the material determines the style of frog you can make. For example, soft braids or cords can be coiled tightly into elaborate frogs, while stiff braids or cords will make simpler frogs. If you enjoy braid work, you can make braids using a variety of plaiting and weaving techniques. Or you can experiment with commercial braids, many of which are composed of multiple smaller braids that can be taken apart and recombined into a frog that uses multiple braids, such as the double spiral (see p. 87).

If you can't find a cord or braid to match your garment, make your own. Almost any fabric, from lightweight silk to heavy velvet, can be used to cover a core, which is sold in a variety of diameters in upholstery sections of fabric stores. To cover the core, cut bias strips of fabric in a width twice the diameter of the core: i.e., for a ⅜-in. diameter core, cut strips ¾ in. wide. Fold the bias strips in half lengthwise, right sides together, and sew the fabric down the center into a long tube. Then turn the tube right-side out over the core.

Some frogs require a continuous loop, so you'll need to splice the cord together to complete the loop. To make a nearly invisible splice, push back the covering at each end of the core and trim 1 in. off each end, as shown in the drawing below. If the core begins to unravel, apply a drop of fray prevention.

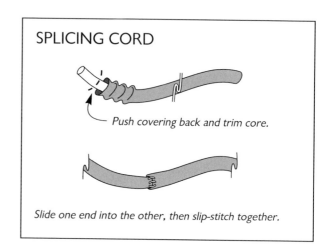

SPLICING CORD

Push covering back and trim core.

Slide one end into the other, then slip-stitch together.

Turn the cut edge of the covering inside by tying a thread around the cut end. Put a needle on the other end of the thread. Pass the needle down the center of the covering near where the thread is tied on and out of the covering about 1 in. down. Pull on the thread and roll the end in your fingers until the tied end slips down inside the covering. Repeat for the other end. Butt the ends together and slip-stitch them. Always try to place the splice in the most inconspicuous spot as you form your frog.

For many of the frogs illustrated here, you'll need to draw a pattern on paper to ensure that both halves will be the same size and shape. Use a copy machine to enlarge or reduce a pattern to the size you want. Place the pattern over foam board or cardboard and shape the frog by pinning the cord or braid to follow the pattern. To determine how much cord or braid you'll need, lay a tape measure on its side and loop it around the pattern, adding about 2 in. for splices.

Skilled seamstresses can form and attach frogs in one step, but you'll probably make the frogs first and apply them later, sewing the frogs twice. As you form frogs, stitch wherever the loops meet or cross to hold the shape temporarily. Then sew the frogs on permanently when the garment is finished. Remember to sew the areas just behind the loop and just behind the button most securely. These are the areas that receive all the stress when the frog is closed.

Looped Frogs

A variety of frogs can be made by looping cord or braid into a pattern. Stiff cords and braids work especially well for the simple, open designs of these frogs because they hold their shapes.

The four looped frogs here are worked from the back, with the right side face down on the board.

Three-leaf clover   EASY

The three-leaf clover is often commercially available but only in white, black, and metallic gold, and in limited sizes. By making your own covered cord (see facing page) for this frog, you can have any color, texture, and size you want.

To make the sample in red and gold on p. 84, you'll need:
- round cord
- foam board or cardboard
- thread
- pins
- needle.

Copy the pattern at the top of p. 85 on a sheet of paper. Place it over the foam board or cardboard and measure to determine how much cord you'll need, plus 2 in. for finishing the ends. Cut the cord and

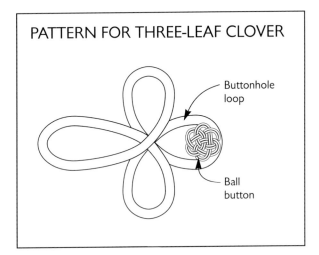

PATTERN FOR THREE-LEAF CLOVER

Buttonhole loop

Ball button

shape it to follow the pattern, placing the ends at the center back to conceal them, and pinning it in position as needed. Stitch wherever loops cross or touch, then stitch the tails down on the back to conceal them.

For the button side, sew a button on the loop after the frog is completed. Another option is to form a ball button (as discussed on pp. 56-58) in your cord about 3 in. from the end, then continue shaping the frog from the rest of the cord. For the buttonhole side, make a loop just large enough to go over the button you've chosen.

Double-loop frog EASY

Each half of the double-loop frog contains both a functional button and a functional loop. Because the loops that go over the buttons are so large, the toggle button (see p. 59) is an excellent choice for this frog. The sample shown here uses a flat braid with a heavy thread along each edge. When the thread is pulled, the braid gathers up along the edge, allowing the braid to be formed into loops while remaining flat. To see whether a braid will do this, test it by pulling a thread along one edge to see if it gathers. Battenberg lace tapes work well for this type of frog.

To make the center sample in gold on the facing page, you'll need:
- flat braid with heavy edge thread
- two toggle buttons
- foam board or cardboard
- thread
- pins
- needle.

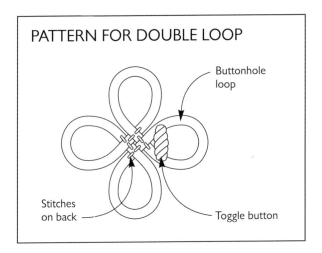

PATTERN FOR DOUBLE LOOP

Buttonhole loop

Stitches on back

Toggle button

Looped frogs: clockwise from upper left, palmate, three-leaf clover, double spiral; in center, double-loop frog.

Trace and pin the pattern shown at the bottom of p. 85 on the foam board or cardboard and measure to determine the cord length, as you did on p. 83. Make two identical loop halves following the pattern. Stitch together where the loops cross. Sew a toggle button (see p. 59) onto each half of the frog at the base of the buttonhole loop near the center of the frog. To close this frog, pull one buttonhole loop through the center of the other loop. Place each loop over the toggle button on the other half.

Palmate frog

EASY

The simple, open pattern of this frog demands a stiff, round cord.

To make the sample in red on p. 84, you'll need:
- stiff round cord
- foam board or cardboard
- thread
- pins
- needle.

Trace the pattern at right and place it over the foam board or cardboard. Measure around the pattern to determine the length of cord you need, and don't forget to add 2 in. for splicing. If you choose to make a ball button (see p. 56-58) in your cord, measure and cut your cord after the ball button has been completed.

Shape the cord to match your pattern, pinning it in place as needed, and place the splice in the most inconspicuous place possible. For the buttonhole side, make a loop just large enough to go over the button. Stitch the cord together wherever it touches.

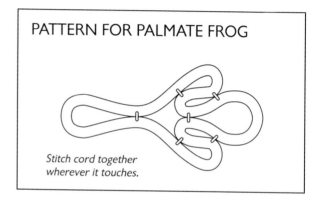

PATTERN FOR PALMATE FROG

Stitch cord together wherever it touches.

Double-spiral frog   MODERATE

The decorative spirals in this frog are formed from a round braid and a round cord, which are looped together. The button and the loop are formed from a separate length of cord (or you can use the braid) and then stitched to the back of the spirals.

To make the bottom sample in gold on p. 84, you'll need:
- round cord
- round braid
- foam board or cardboard
- thread
- pins
- needle.

   To make two identical spirals, draw and pin the pattern at right to the board. Measure to determine the length of the cord and the braid and add 2 in. Hold the braid and the cord together, placing the cord to the inside of the braid, and form the pattern. Pin the loops in position, stitch them together everywhere they cross or touch, and stitch the cord to the braid as needed. Finish by stitching the tails down so that they won't show on the front.

With either the cord or the braid, make a ball button (see p. 56-58), leaving long tails. You may need to repeat each round of the ball button three times to make it large enough for the frog. Again using either the cord or braid and leaving tails, make a loop just large enough to go over the button. Determine the placement of the button and the loop, and then stitch the tails to the back of each side of the frog.

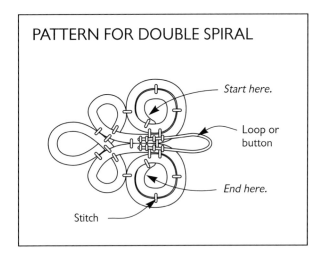

PATTERN FOR DOUBLE SPIRAL

Start here.

Loop or button

End here.

Stitch

Decorative Knots

Decorative knots make beautiful, intricate frogs. You'll find patterns for three knots here, and two books will be helpful if you wish to design your own knotted frogs. *The Encyclopedia of Knots and Fancy Rope Work* shows how to make many different knots that can be used for frogs. *Celtic Knotwork* will show you how to design an endless knot to fit any size and shape (see Helpful Books on p. 109). The decorative knots in this section will be worked from the front.

Double-knot frog
EASY

The double-knot frog will be centered and sewn on the overlapping front edge of a garment. You'll need to secure the frog, then position and attach the buttons. Only the button on the underlap side is functional.

To make the sample in aqua blue at left, you'll need:
- cord
- two buttons
- thread
- needle.

Cut the cord five to six times the length of the finished frog (see p. 83 to find out how to determine the length). Loop the cord, stitching or taping the two ends together. Wrap a figure-eight knot according to the pattern below. Adjust the knot so that the frog is the right length and the tails are hidden on the back. Stitch the cord to itself to hold the frogs together, and stitch the tails down.

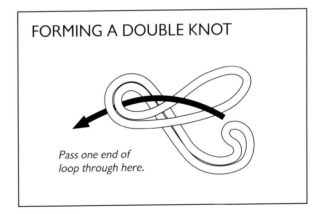

FORMING A DOUBLE KNOT

Pass one end of loop through here.

Decorative-knot frogs: from top to bottom, flat weave, fishes, double knot.

Flat-weave frog

MODERATE

The flat-weave frog is the same knot as the Turk's-head knot. The flat weave is a versatile frog that can be made with one, two, three, or more rounds of loops. It's possible to position the knot to form a square or a diamond, or pull on two opposite sets of loops to enlarge them and form a long, thin frog. You can leave spaces between the loops and the center crisscross pattern so that the underlying fabric shows through, or you can tighten up the loops so that there are no spaces.

To make the sample in teal blue on p. 88, you'll need:
- 3 yd. of rattail cord
- foam board or cardboard
- thread
- pins
- needle
- transparent tape.

Copy the outer shape of the pattern below on a sheet of paper and place it on the board. Wrap tape around one end of the cord to make weaving the knot easier. Make a ball button in one end of the rattail, or attach a bead or button later. Pin the button (or a 4-in. length of the cord for the loop) to the start position on the pattern.

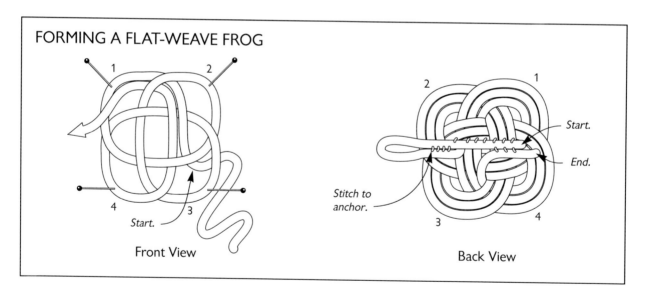

FORMING A FLAT-WEAVE FROG

Front View

Back View

90

To form the outer round of the knot, form loops 1 and 2 following the pattern. At loops 3 and 4, begin the weaving pattern. Remember the rule for weaving: When forming an odd-numbered loop, weave over the sides of even-numbered loops and under the sides of other odd-numbered loops; for an even-numbered loop, weave over the sides of odd-numbered loops and under the sides of other even-numbered loops.

To form the second and third round of loops, trace inside the route of the first round. Adjust the knot so that it lies flat and does not have any large gaps between the loops. Stitch the ends down on the back and stitch loops together so that the frog will hold its shape until sewn onto your garment.

Fishes

MODERATE

The fish frog can have a variety of looks. If the herringbone wraps are pulled tightly, they'll form a line instead of the V in the sample shown here. Round braids and cords will create quite a different look from the flat soutache braid, which is angled in different directions to emphasize the pattern. And you can easily change the size of the finished frog by increasing or decreasing the number of wraps.

To make the samples in yellow and blue on p. 88, you'll need:
- 4 ft. of soutache braid
- foam board or cardboard
- thread
- pins
- needle
- transparent tape.

Copy the outer shape of the pattern below on a piece of paper and place it on a board. Tape one end of braid to make weaving easier. Make a ball button in one end of the braid for the button half.

If you use soutache, or any flat braid, you'll need to stand it on edge as you pull it around the pins to shape the loop pattern, then lay it flat as you weave the herringbone pattern across top and back. This is not necessary if you use round braid.

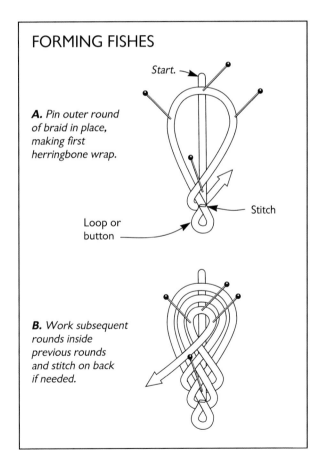

FORMING FISHES

Start.

A. Pin outer round of braid in place, making first herringbone wrap.

Stitch

Loop or button

B. Work subsequent rounds inside previous rounds and stitch on back if needed.

To weave the pattern, position the ball button (or the button loop when making the buttonhole half) at the lower pin and insert four pins in the outer perimeter as marked (see drawing on p. 91). With the braid on edge, wrap around the upper three pins. To make the first herringbone pattern, lay the braid flat and work around the outside of the lower pin: across the front, around the back, and across the front again. Again, stand the braid on edge and wrap another loop inside the first, using three more pins to hold the loop in place. Turn the braid flat again and wrap another herringbone pattern inside the lower pin and toward the center: cross the front, the back, and then the front again, as shown in drawing B on p. 91. Repeat for six rounds, always working toward the center.

To finish the last round, tuck the braid tail through the center of the top loops. Stitch on the back to hold the flat wraps in place, to secure the top loops in place, and to keep the tail hidden.

Spirals

The spiral frogs shown on the facing page are formed from spirals and loops arranged to make different designs. The designs are used extensively on traditional Chinese blouses and jackets. The spirals, which are reminiscent of paper quilling, are usually made from $\frac{3}{16}$-in. or $\frac{1}{4}$-in. satin bias tape, but other flat and round braids can be used.

The drawback with satin bias tape is that it is not available commercially: You'll have to make it yourself, but that's not difficult to do. Start with $\frac{3}{4}$ yd. of satin fabric. To make $\frac{1}{4}$-in. bias tape, cut the fabric into 1-in. wide bias strips. Fold each strip in half lengthwise and press the fold. Turn the raw edge on one side into the fold and press the fold in place. Repeat with the other raw edge. Machine-stitch the open edge closed $\frac{1}{16}$ in. from the edge. The stitched edge will be the wrong side of the frog and will be hidden next to the garment.

The spiral frogs here are worked from the back. I find it helpful to copy the pattern and use it as a guide to make sure both halves are the same size. After you've made a few of these frogs, you might find it easier to work them in your hand rather than flat on the paper, occasionally comparing the size to the pattern.

Spiral frogs: flower (top), snail (bottom).

Snails

EASY

To make the sample in white on p. 93, you'll need:
- two 2-ft. lengths of satin bias tape
- thread
- needle.

In the center of one of the satin strips, make a ball button (see pp. 56-58), using only one round of loops. Cut both tails to 6 in. Fold the tip of the tape under to hide the tail, and roll it into a spiral, stitching the tape to itself every ¼ in. or so along the machine-stitching line, as shown in the drawing at right. Repeat for the other tail. For the buttonhole half of the frog, form a loop in another length of satin bias tape that will just fit over the button, and stitch the loop in place. Trim the tails to 6 in. and complete the spirals in the same manner as the first half of the frog.

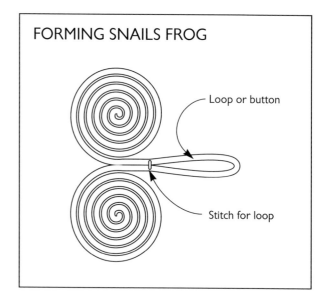

FORMING SNAILS FROG

Loop or button

Stitch for loop

Flower

MODERATE

To make the sample in yellow on p. 93, you'll need:
- two 2-ft. lengths of soutache braid
- thread
- needle.

For the button half, make a ball button (see pp. 56-58) in the center of the soutache braid using one round of loops.

Cut one end to 3 in. Fold the tip of the braid to hide the raw edge at the back of the frog. Beginning at the folded tip of the shorter end, roll the braid into a spiral, stitching the braid to itself every ¼ in. or so along the centerline of the braid (see drawing at right). Stop about 1½ in. from the button. Using the other tail and starting near the ball button, form 11 loops one at a time, stitching evenly around the outer round of the spiral as each one is formed. Cut the tail and stitch it to the back of the spiral. For the other half of the frog, form a loop in the other length of soutache braid that will just fit over the button and stitch the loop in place. Complete the spiral and loops in the same manner as the first half of the frog.

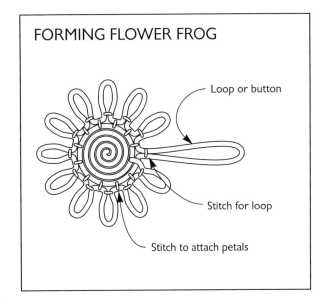

FORMING FLOWER FROG

Loop or button

Stitch for loop

Stitch to attach petals

Fabric and Ribbon Buttons

Here is a group of bold, playful buttons that you can make quickly and easily. The fabrics and the ribbons used for these buttons can range from simple gingham checks to elegant velvets and silks, and the results can be whimsical or dramatic. These buttons are made on or applied to molds that are readily available in almost any fabric store.

Fabric- and ribbon-covered buttons were introduced in the early 1800s and became the fashion rage by the middle of the century. Women wore rows of tiny self-fabric buttons (buttons made from the same fabric as the garment) down the front and on the sleeves of their dresses and jackets. Seamstresses and tailors could find commercial molds and easily make buttons to match the fabric of the garments they were sewing. By Victorian times, intricately designed ribbons woven in multiple colors were mass-produced specifically for buttons.

Tailored Buttons

The four buttons in this group are often used on tailored jackets and dresses in matching or coordinating fabric. They tend to be understated and can look quite elegant. They're just right when you don't want a button to call attention to itself.

But don't limit yourself to matching fabrics. Try mixing instead. Choose a bold motif from a ribbon, a brocade, or even a man's tie. When making these buttons from patterned fabrics or ribbons, take time to consider the placement of the fabric motifs on the button. Cut a circle in a piece of cardboard the same diameter as the button you want and move it around the fabric to view different sections of the fabric as they would appear on the buttons. I bring cardboard cutouts in various diameters to the fabric store to help select fabrics for buttons.

Covered-mold buttons   `EASY`

Buttons made from self-fabric and a commercial mold are easy to make. Here are a few tips that will help you get better results.

To make the silk brocade buttons on the facing page, you'll need:
- #45 flat commercial mold
- silk brocade
- quilting thread
- needle.

Cut out a circle of fabric (or ribbon) according to the instructions on the package, or twice the diameter of the mold. If the mold will show through the fabric, cut a liner the same size as the fabric out of lightweight, tightly woven fabric. Hold the two together and treat them as one. To cover the mold, follow the directions on pp. 10-11. Adjust the gathers around the outer edge, check the position of the design on the front so that you can place the shank correctly, and then attach the back. For professional-looking buttons, use a covered commercial back (see p. 12).

If you are using something else for a mold, like a disk or an old button, cut the fabric twice the diameter of the mold and follow the directions on pp. 10-11. Choose an appropriate back (see pp. 12-13), check the direction you want the shank to go, and then work the back.

Tailored buttons: clockwise from upper left, plaited buttons, Singletons, covered-mold buttons, rimmed buttons.

Singleton

The Singleton is a fabric-covered Dorset button. This style of button was made exclusively by the Singleton family in the late 1600s, and like other Dorset buttons, was made over a ring. The traditional Singleton was white. It used a blanket stitch or a backstitch to capture the ring and had a small, five-petaled, lazy daisy flower embroidered on top. (Some black Singletons were produced as mourning buttons.) The original button was tiny, about ½ in. in diameter, but it can be made in any size and in a wide range of fabric weights. The button can be very discreet if made plain in self-fabric, or very elaborate if embellished with embroidery or beads.

To make the sample in red and white on p. 98, you'll need:
- ¾-in. ring
- light- to medium-weight fabric
- quilting thread
- needle.

Cut a 1¾-in. circle of fabric (about two and a half times the diameter of the ring). With quilting thread, run a gathering stitch ⅛ in. from the outer edge of the fabric. Place the ring in the center of the fabric. Pull up the thread to gather the fabric over the ring. Tuck the outer raw edge of the fabric to the inside using the tip of your scissors. This will pad the center of the button and give it some height. If you want more height, add a little stuffing—fabric scraps or polyester batting will work. Tie the thread but don't cut it off. With the same thread, work a herringbone stitch (see p. 10) around the back of button to pull the fabric tight over the ring, close the back, and neaten the center back. Again, tie off the thread but don't cut it.

Next, secure the ring so that it can't slip inside the fabric covering. On the front, work one round of backstitches (see the drawing below) just inside the ring, or work one round of blanket stitches over the ring. To finish the back, make a woven shank (see p. 13) using quilting thread.

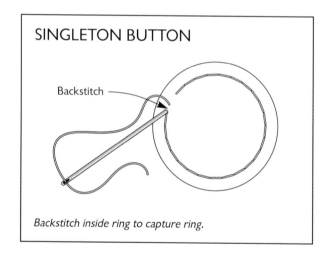

SINGLETON BUTTON

Backstitch

Backstitch inside ring to capture ring.

Rimmed buttons `EASY`

Rimmed button molds are available with either gold- or silver-tone rims (see the Supply List on p. 108). If you can't find rimmed molds, use rimmed earring kits and add a back from a commercial button mold.

Rimmed molds are excellent for mounting ribbon motifs because you don't have to gather the ribbon around the back of the mold top. Flat objects, such as coins, stamps, or small photographs, can be mounted in the rims also.

To make the gold-rimmed buttons on p. 98, you'll need:
- #45 rimmed button mold
- 1 in. of 1-in. wide ribbon to cover center
- quilting thread
- needle.

Select and center a pleasing motif from your ribbon. Follow the package directions to cover the ring. The mold will snap over the circle of the ribbon easily; you won't need to gather the fabric.

Sometimes you may want to cover the rims with fabric, too. If you try this, use a commercial covered back and stitch the back in place; otherwise, the additional fabric covering the rim will prevent the button back from snapping into place.

To make the navy-blue rimmed button on p. 98, you'll need:
- #45 rimmed button mold
- lightweight fabric to cover rim
- coordinating fabric or 1-in. wide ribbon to cover center
- quilting thread
- needle.

To cover the rim, cut a ¾-in. wide bias strip of fabric long enough to go around the outside edge of the rim, plus ¼ in. Stitch the ends together, keeping a ⅛-in. seam allowance. Press the seam open and turn the bias-strip circle right-side out. Slip the rim inside the bias circle and fold the raw edges over the rim so that they meet at the back. Stitch the raw edges together next to the rim. Cover the top of the mold following the package directions and slip the mold inside the rim. Make a fabric covering for the back that came with button mold (see p. 12). Fold the raw edges of the rim fabric toward center. Center the back over the rim and then stitch the back to the rim fabric.

Plaited ribbon buttons `EASY`

Ribbon can be plaited, woven, or braided to create interesting color and texture combinations on buttons. By picking up colors and textures from the garment, a plaited button can unify different design aspects of the garment.

You may use many different weaving patterns. On p. 98 is a simple four-ribbon pattern that uses two different ribbons. Finer ribbons can be woven into checkerboard, tumbling block, or braided patterns.

To make the samples in pink or blue on p. 98, you'll need:

- #45 half-round commercial button mold
- 1-in. wide satin ribbon
- 1-in. wide grosgrain ribbon
- sheer fusible interfacing
- quilting thread
- needle.

Cut a 2½-in. square of interfacing and place it on an ironing board adhesive-side up. Cut two 3-in. lengths of satin ribbon and two 3-in. lengths of grosgrain ribbon for each button. Working on top of the interfacing, weave the basket pattern, alternating grosgrain and satin ribbon. Carefully pull each ribbon out so that it laps under the previous length by about ¼ in. This will allow you to fuse all layers securely. (The tails will be cut off when you trim to the pattern size.) Pin the ribbons to the interfacing, if necessary, then fuse following interfacing directions.

To keep the ribbons from pulling apart when the back is snapped on the button, work a tight X with quilting thread at the center where the ribbons meet. Trim the design to size using the pattern that came with the mold. Work a running stitch around the outside of the circle and gather the circle over the mold top. Center the design, check shank alignment, and snap on the back.

Floral Buttons

Ribbon and fabric can be manipulated by folding, pleating, gathering, and twisting to make eye-catching buttons. These buttons tend to be large to show off the lovely textures and patterns created. Ribbons have the advantage of having a strong yet small selvage that doesn't require turning under. When manipulating fabric for floral buttons, you either have to double the fabric or turn an edge, so the edge won't show, and the fabric won't ravel.

Fabric flowers   EASY

The most gorgeous fabric flowers that I recall are those on Baltimore quilts. The book *Dimensional Appliqué, Baskets, Blooms, and Baltimore Borders: A Pattern Companion* (see Helpful Books on p. 109) describes techniques for many fabric and ribbon flowers that can be adapted to buttons.

To make beautiful fabric flower buttons, keep these tips in mind. Use sheer or lightweight fabric: organza, china silk, and batiste work well. Keep raw edges to the underside by folding the fabric in half. Sometimes it's helpful to finish raw edges with a tiny rolled hem, or by serging, which may allow you to use fabric for patterns that call for ribbons. And when you're forming the flowers, always keep the center of the underside spread out so that you don't form a hard lump at the center back.

Floral buttons: clockwise from upper left, rosette, fabric flowers, Soho twist; in center, ribbon flowers.

To make the sample in pink on p. 103, you'll need:
- #45 flat commercial button mold
- silk charmeuse fabric
- quilting thread
- needle.

Cut a bias strip of silk 1½ in. by 20 in. and fold it in half lengthwise. Holding the raw edges together, work a running stitch along the edge, and then gather lightly along the running stitches. Fold one end down at 45° to hide the tail and begin rolling the fabric into a spiral, stitching as necessary to secure your work. As you roll, pull gathers tighter and tighter to form petals. After the first round or two, move the bottom edge up about ¼ in. from the bottom of the previous round before stitching the gathered edge down. Continue moving up as you complete the flower, as shown in the drawing at right. Turn the end down at 45° to hide the raw edge, and stitch it in place.

Cover the mold with silk, following the instructions for covered molds; use more than one layer of fabric if necessary. To position the flower on the mold, take two or three stitches through the fabric at the center of the mold and the center of the flower. Then move to the outer edge of the mold and stitch the back of the outer petal to the outer edge of the mold all the way around.

FABRIC FLOWER

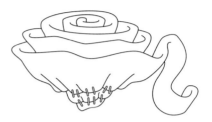

Spiral out from center. After two rounds or so, move up about ¼ in. on previous petal before stitching petal in place.

Ribbon flowers

`EASY`

The books *Dimensional Appliqué, Baskets, Blooms, and Baltimore Borders* and *The Art and Craft of Ribbon Work* (see Helpful Books on p. 109) illustrate the techniques of making flowers and cockades, as well as other ribbon motifs—not necessarily flowers—all of which would make great buttons.

For really fast ribbon flower buttons, buy premade ribbon flowers and stitch (or glue) them to fabric-covered molds. Use a mold that's a half to two-thirds the width of the ribbon flower so that the mold does not show.

To make the sample in mauve on p. 103, you'll need:

- #30 flat commercial button mold
- ⅜-in. single-sided satin ribbon: 18 in. for the flower, 4 in. for the leaves
- fabric
- quilting thread
- needle.

Cut the ribbon for the flower and the leaves, using two different-colored ribbons. Form and stitch ½-in. wide box pleats along the 18-in. length, as shown in the drawing at right. To form the flower, roll the pleated ribbon into a spiral, stitching together along one edge as necessary. Fold the remaining end down and stitch it in place. Loop the 4-in. length of ribbon into a figure eight to form the leaves, stitching to secure at center. Position the leaves behind the flower and stitch the two together at the center back of the flower.

Cover the mold with fabric that matches the leaves, following the instructions on pp. 10-11. Take two or three stitches through the fabric on the mold and then through the center back of the flower. Move to the outer edge of the mold. Pull the outer pleats—one at a time—down to the mold and stitch the pleats to the fabric around the mold.

RIBBON FLOWER

Fold and stitch near edge to form box pleats, which will later form flower.

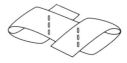

Fold and stitch to form the leaf.

Soho twist

MODERATE

To create the Soho twist, ribbon is looped, twisted, and stitched directly to the button mold to create a beautiful and unusual button.

To make the sample in ecru on p. 103, you'll need:
- #45 half-dome commercial button mold
- silk fabric
- ¼-in. silk ribbon
- quilting thread
- needle.

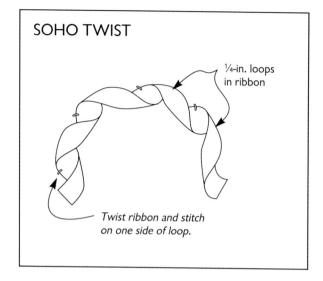

SOHO TWIST

¼-in. loops in ribbon

Twist ribbon and stitch on one side of loop.

Begin by covering the mold with silk fabric to match your ribbon (follow instructions on pp. 10-11). Use two or three layers of fabric, if necessary, to cover the mold completely.

To anchor your thread and position the center of the flower, take a small stitch through the fabric at the center of the mold. Lay the tail of the silk ribbon at center and take one stitch on each side of the ribbon. Make a ¼-in. circular loop in the ribbon and stitch again on each side. Make one twist in the ribbon, keeping a ¼-in. high loop. Lay this loop next to the center loop and stitch it in place with one stitch on the side toward the outer edge of the mold, as shown in the drawing at right. Continue twisting and stitching, laying the twists down in an outward spiraling pattern and always keeping about a ¼-in. high loop in the ribbon. At the end, cut the ribbon, fold the end under ⅛ in., and stitch it in place.

Rosette

EASY

This button looks complicated (see p. 103), but it's one of the easiest to make. The sample I've made is formed from a loop braid that has loops stitched together near one edge. These braids are sometimes easier to find in upholstery stores than in fabric stores. If you can't find a loop braid in a color you want, any 1-in. wide ribbon can be gathered or pleated and substituted for the loop braid.

To make the sample in lavender on p. 103, you'll need:
• 1-yd. of loop braid, ½ in. to 1 in. wide
• thread
• buckram (optional)
• needle.

Roll the braid into a circular snail shape and stitch it together about every ½ in. along the stitching line of the braid. When the circle is the size you want for your finished button, cut the braid, and stitch the tail under.

If the button is firm enough, add the back you want, and you're done. If you need a firmer base, stitch or glue a circle of buckram to the base, or sew on a covered commercial back if you need a shank.

Resources

Supply List

Britex
146 Geary St.
San Francisco, CA 94108
(415) 392 -2910
Gimp, soutache braid

Burgess Manufacturing Corp.
Maxtant Division
3600 Windsor Park Dr.
Suwanee (Atlanta), GA 30174
(404) 932-1111 in GA,
(800) 662-5551 outside GA
Maxtant rimmed button molds
    (wholesale only; call for
    distributors)

Cherry Tree Toys, Inc.
P.O. Box 369
Belmont, OH 43718-0369
(800) 848-4363
Half-domed wood molds
    (miniature wheels),
    high-domed wood molds
    (hub caps)

Cope & Timmins, Ltd.
Angel Road Works
Edmonton, London N18 3AY
081-803 6481
Hollow brass rings, ½ in. to
    1¼ in.

Eastern Findings Corp.
19 West 34th St.
New York, NY 10001
(212) 695-6640
Seamless brass rings, ½ in. to
    1 in. (wholesale only)

Helby Import Co.
74 Rupert Ave.
Staten Island, NY 10314
(718) 447-0008
Griffin silk bead cord, 19 colors,
    sizes 0 to 16

**Japanese Embroidery Center:
    Kurenai-Kai, Ltd.**
2727 Spalding Dr.
Dunwoody, GA 30350
(404) 390-0617
Japanese flat embroidery silk

Lace Buttons
P.O. Box 2892
Sunnyvale, CA 94087
(408) 984-2558
Threads, braids, molds,
    supplies, kits

Lacis
2982 Adeline St.
Berkeley, CA 94703
(510) 843-7178
Linen lace-making thread,
    cotton tulle

Lin-Wood Products Corp.
506 Oakland Ave. SW
Grand Rapids, MI 49503
(800) 458-1578
High-domed wood molds
    (hub caps)

Shay Pendray's Needle Arts, Inc.
2211 Monroe
Dearborn, MI 48124
(313) 278-6266
Japanese flat embroidery silk

YLI Corp.
45 West 300 North
Provo, UT 84601
(801) 377-3900
Kanagawa silk embroidery
    thread (1000 denier) (#16),
    211 colors, will match fabric
    swatch
Kanagawa silk buttonhole twist,
    83 colors, ¼-in. silk ribbon
Candelight metallic yarn,
    20 colors

Helpful Books

The Art and Craft of Ribbon Work edited by Jules Kliot and Kaethe Kliot. Lacis Publications, Berkeley, CA, 1993.

Celtic Knotwork by Iain Bain. Sterling Publishing Co., New York, NY, 1994.

Dimensional Appliqué, Baskets, Blooms, and Baltimore Borders: A Pattern Companion by Elly Sienkiewicz. C & T Publishing, Martinez, CA, 1993.

Dorset Buttons-Fact File (booklet) by Marion Howitt. "Swanston," Russell Ave., Swanage, Dorset, BH192EB, England.

The Encyclopedia of Knots and Fancy Rope Work by Raoul Graumont and John Hensel. Cornell Maritime Press, 4th edition, Centerville, MD, 1990.

The Harmony Guide to Crocheting: Techniques and Stitches by Debra Mountford. Crown Publication Group, New York, NY, 1993.

McCalls Big Book of Needlecrafts. Chilton Book Co., Radnor, PA, 1982 (out of print).

Teneriffe Lace edited by Jules Kliot and Kaethe Kliot. Lacis Publications, Berkeley, CA, 1993.

Index

Index

Button Index

Photography: Marcus Tullis
Stylist: Sheila Shulman
Editor: Thomas C. McKenna
Designer/Layout Artist: Christopher Casey
Illustrator: Scott Bricher

Typeface: Berkeley Old Style/Giltus
Paper: S.D. Warren, 70# Patina
Printer: Quebecor Printing, Kingsport, Tennessee